Hands-On Cloud Solutions with Azure

Architecting, developing, and deploying the Azure way

Greg Leonardo

BIRMINGHAM - MUMBAI

Hands-On Cloud Solutions with Azure

Commissioning Editor: Vijin Boricha
Acquisition Editor: Prachi Bisht
Content Development Editor: Priyanka Deshpande
Technical Editor: Mohit Hassija
Copy Editor: Safis Editing
Project Coordinator: Drashti Panchal
Proofreader: Safis Editing
Indexer: Pratik Shirodkar
Graphics: Tom Scaria
Production Coordinator: Arvindkumar Gupta

First published: October 2018

Production reference: 1311018

Published by Packt Publishing Ltd.
Livery Place
35 Livery Street
Birmingham
B3 2PB, UK.

ISBN 978-1-78646-865-9

www.packtpub.com

`mapt.io`

Mapt is an online digital library that gives you full access to over 5,000 books and videos, as well as industry leading tools to help you plan your personal development and advance your career. For more information, please visit our website.

Why subscribe?

- Spend less time learning and more time coding with practical eBooks and Videos from over 4,000 industry professionals

- Improve your learning with Skill Plans built especially for you

- Get a free eBook or video every month

- Mapt is fully searchable

- Copy and paste, print, and bookmark content

Packt.com

Did you know that Packt offers eBook versions of every book published, with PDF and ePub files available? You can upgrade to the eBook version at `www.packt.com` and as a print book customer, you are entitled to a discount on the eBook copy. Get in touch with us at `customercare@packtpub.com` for more details.

At `www.packt.com`, you can also read a collection of free technical articles, sign up for a range of free newsletters, and receive exclusive discounts and offers on Packt books and eBooks.

Contributors

About the author

Greg Leonardo has been working in the IT industry since his time in the military. He is a father, veteran, developer, teacher, speaker, Azure MVP, and an early adopter. He has have worked in many facets of IT throughout his career. He is president of #TampaCC, a community meetup, that runs #TampaCC, Azure User Group, Azure Medics, and various technology events throughout Tampa.

I would like to thank my wife, Kate, and my two sons, Maddux and Lucas, for giving me the freedom to pursue sharing my experiences through this book.

About the reviewers

Gajanan Chandgadkar has more than 12 years' experience in the IT sector. He has spent over 6 years in the USA helping large enterprises architect, migrate, and deploy applications in AWS and Azure. He's been running production workloads on AWS for over 6 years, and on Azure for the past year. He is a certified solutions architect professional and a certified DevOps professional with over seven certifications in trending technologies. Gajanan is also a technology enthusiast who has extended his interest and experiences to include different topics, such as application development, container technology, and continuous delivery.

He is currently working with Happiest Minds Technologies as a DevOps architect, having worked with Wipro Technologies Corporation in the past.

Rohit Prakash is an Azure solutions engineer, with an unabashed fondness for Windows and Microsoft Azure in both disciplines. He specializes in Azure IaaS/PaaS design and implementation. In the past, he has made several contributions to Microsoft Community by contributing to TechNet articles, with a focus on Azure. He has been a member of the Microsoft BizSpark program since his college days and he has also been offered an MSDN subscription by Microsoft. He loves writing blogs as a way of sharing his thoughts.

He works with Fujitsu Consulting India and lives in Noida, India, where his personal time is split evenly between family and friends. He enjoys visiting peaceful and devotional locations.

Packt is searching for authors like you

If you're interested in becoming an author for Packt, please visit `authors.packtpub.com` and apply today. We have worked with thousands of developers and tech professionals, just like you, to help them share their insight with the global tech community. You can make a general application, apply for a specific hot topic that we are recruiting an author for, or submit your own idea.

Table of Contents

Preface

This book will focus on addressing the architectural decisions that usually arise when you are designing or migrating a solution to Microsoft Azure. It will start by designing the building blocks of infrastructure solution on Azure, such as Azure compute, storage, and networking, and will then explore the database options available in Microsoft Azure. You will get to grips with designing scalable web and mobile solutions and understand where to host your Active Directory/Identity solution. Moving on, you will find out how to extend your DevOps to Azure. You will benefit from some exciting services that enable extremely smooth operations and streamlined DevOps between on-premises and the cloud. The book will help you design a secure environment for your solution, whether on the cloud or hybrid. Toward the end, it will show you how to manage and monitor cloud and hybrid solutions. This book will arm you with all the tools and knowledge you need to properly plan and design your solution on Azure, whether it's a brand new project or a migration project.

Who this book is for

If you're an IT consultant, developer, or solutions architect looking to design effective solutions for your organization, this book is for you. Some knowledge of cloud computing will assist with understanding the key concepts covered in this book.

What this book covers

Chapter 1, *Getting Started with Azure*, covers the things that are important when getting started with Azure.

Chapter 2, *Moving Existing Apps to Azure*, includes lifting, shifting, or migrating the apps and understanding how to get the existing apps to Azure.

Chapter 3, *Building Solutions in Azure*, covers the things you need to know about building and developing solutions in Azure.

Chapter 4, *Understanding the Infrastructure behind Solutions Built in Azure*, explains how to leverage ARM templates and infrastructure-as-code, and helps with adopting standards to provide guidance on resource usage in Azure.

Chapter 5, *Developing Solutions the Right Way in Azure*, explains how to develop solutions in Azure, things you have to trust, guidance on selecting the type of resources to develop, and explains how to leverage application insights in your application development to help with application monitoring and support.

Chapter 6, *Deploying Solutions to Azure*, covers the things you need to know about deploying solutions in Azure.

Chapter 7, *Putting it All Together*, includes monitoring and supporting applications and troubleshooting issues.

Chapter 8, *Best Practices to Make Your Life Easier in Azure*, includes some best practices and tips on making your life easier in Azure and covers development practices in connection with dashboards and monitoring.

To get the most out of this book

Some basic knowledge of cloud computing would come in handy. A knowledge of other Azure services would be a bonus.

Download the example code files

You can download the example code files for this book from your account at www.packt.com. If you purchased this book elsewhere, you can visit www.packt.com/support and register to have the files emailed directly to you.

You can download the code files by following these steps:

1. Log in or register at www.packt.com.
2. Select the **SUPPORT** tab.
3. Click on **Code Downloads & Errata**.
4. Enter the name of the book in the **Search** box and follow the onscreen instructions.

Once the file is downloaded, please make sure that you unzip or extract the folder using the latest version of:

- WinRAR/7-Zip for Windows
- Zipeg/iZip/UnRarX for Mac
- 7-Zip/PeaZip for Linux

The code bundle for the book is also hosted on GitHub at `https://github.com/PacktPublishing/Hands-On-Cloud-Solutions-with-Azure`. In case there's an update to the code, it will be updated on the existing GitHub repository.

We also have other code bundles from our rich catalog of books and videos available at `https://github.com/PacktPublishing/`. Check them out!

Download the color images

We also provide a PDF file that has color images of the screenshots/diagrams used in this book. You can download it here: `https://www.packtpub.com/sites/default/files/downloads/9781786468659_ColorImages.pdf`.

Conventions used

There are a number of text conventions used throughout this book.

`CodeInText`: Indicates code words in text, database table names, folder names, filenames, file extensions, pathnames, dummy URLs, user input, and Twitter handles. Here is an example: "The `parameters` are the input to the template and are the values that are provided by the `parameters` file."

A block of code is set as follows:

```
{
    "$schema":
"http://schema.management.azure.com/schemas/2015-01-01/deploymentTemplate.json#",        "contentVersion": "",
    "parameters": { },
    "variables": { },
    "functions": { },
    "resources": [ ],
    "outputs": { }
}
```

Any command-line input or output is written as follows:

```
Login-AzureRmAccount
```

Bold: Indicates a new term, an important word, or words that you see on screen. For example, words in menus or dialog boxes appear in the text like this. Here is an example: "Enter an **App Name**, **Subscription**, **Resource Group Name**, and **Database Provider** to **Azure Database for MySQL**."

Warnings or important notes appear like this.

 Tips and tricks appear like this.

Get in touch

Feedback from our readers is always welcome.

General feedback: Email customercare@packtpub.com and mention the book title in the subject of your message. If you have questions about any aspect of this book, please email us at customercare@packtpub.com.

Errata: Although we have taken every care to ensure the accuracy of our content, mistakes do happen. If you have found a mistake in this book, we would be grateful if you would report this to us. Please visit www.packt.com/submit-errata, selecting your book, clicking on the Errata Submission Form link, and entering the details.

Piracy: If you come across any illegal copies of our works in any form on the internet, we would be grateful if you would provide us with the location address or website name. Please contact us at copyright@packt.com with a link to the material.

If you are interested in becoming an author: If there is a topic that you have expertise in, and you are interested in either writing or contributing to a book, please visit authors.packtpub.com.

Reviews

Please leave a review. Once you have read and used this book, why not leave a review on the site that you purchased it from? Potential readers can then see and use your unbiased opinion to make purchase decisions, we at Packt can understand what you think about our products, and our authors can see your feedback on their book. Thank you!

For more information about Packt, please visit packt.com.

Getting Started with Azure

1

In this chapter, we will learn how to set up our virtual organization called the **tenant**, understand how to access it, and what elements make up our Azure experience. We will learn the differences and boundaries between a tenant, subscription, and resource groups. Then, we will cover how to leverage the marketplace to provide quick solutions through the portal and understand common terminology.

In this chapter, we will be covering the following topics:

- Getting started with Azure
- How I started using Azure
- Understanding the role of the marketplace in Azure
- Common Azure terminology used when using the portal

Technical requirements

There are no technical requirements for this chapter, but these are important links you should review:

- Azure portal: `https://portal.azure.com/`
- Azure Resource Limits: `https://docs.microsoft.com/en-us/azure/azure-subscription-service-limits`
- Azure Pricing Calculator: `https://azure.microsoft.com/en-us/pricing/calculator/`
- Azure Connect: `https://docs.microsoft.com/en-us/azure/active-directory/connect/active-directory-aadconnect`
- Azure Active Directory Pricing: `https://azure.microsoft.com/en-us/pricing/details/active-directory/`

- **Azure Marketplace Labs:** `https://azuremarketplace.microsoft.com/en-us/marketplace/?source=datamarket`
- **Private Cloud:** `https://azure.microsoft.com/en-us/overview/what-is-a-private-cloud/`

What is cloud computing?

It is the delivery of computer services over the internet to assist with resource flexibility, scale, and innovation. These services include servers/VMs, physical storage, data repositories, networking resources, analytics, software, and more. These services are offered at a much smaller pay-for-use model than physical data centers and organizations generally migrate to the compute service model for the following reasons:

- **Global** allows an organization to scale elastically and allow regional entry points, providing a more consistent experience for their user base
- **Speed** allows the faster provision of resources and helps release pressure on capacity planning because it removed the need to order and wait for resources
- **Cost** is simplified into a pay-as-you-go model, removing the capital expense over the physical resources
- **Security** is provided through an extensive set of policies and controls that strengthen your overall security posture
- **Productivity** is increased by removing a significant number of tasks, such as hardware setup, patching, and other operational management chores
- **Performance** is achieved through worldwide distribution of services and is regularly updated to the latest generation of computing hardware

Cloud computing comes in private, public, and hybrid types, with each offering its own benefits:

- **Public clouds** are generally owned by third parties such as Amazon, Microsoft, and Google, who control all the supporting infrastructure, hardware, and software
- **Private clouds** are owned by a business and maintained on a private network
- **Hybrid clouds** are combinations of public and private, as well as on-premise resources

But at the end of the day, what problems do clouds solve? Let's understand this in the following section.

What problems does it solve?

The biggest benefit of the cloud is it allows organizations to expand without a large capital cost, and also allows new/small businesses to shrink their startup or capital into a pay-as-you-go model. The cloud allows for innovation to happen without the traditional fears of infrastructure purchases, giving the ability to bring up and tear down in a rapid and cost effective way with little concern for the infrastructure needed.

Think of it as an unlimited playground where the only true limit is your imagination. You can now build, migrate, or rebuild your applications, so you truly only have to worry about the application and not about everything around it. So, the problem it solves is allowing your organization to scale faster, while controlling cost and offline responsibilities to help streamline IT operations.

The cloud targets not only development but operational resources, allowing you to focus on the things that truly matter to an organization. It fosters increased communication between all facets of the organization, from requirement gathering to automated deployment and testing. Let's take a look at Microsoft's cloud solution, Azure.

What is Azure?

Azure is Microsoft's cloud offering, which comes in private, on-premise (Azure Stack), government, and public versions (refer to this link for further details `https://azure.microsoft.com/en-us/overview/what-is-a-private-cloud/`). It was announced on October 2008, released on February 2010, and is the next evolution of virtualization. The *magic* of Azure is built on top of a technology called Service Fabric and Fabric controllers; it works as a distributed application system that handles the allocation of servers or services, monitors the health of these, and heals them as needed. Each Fabric Controller orchestrates all the resources needed within the Azure platform. All the network resources and servers have been abstracted out of your view and there is no longer a need to support and maintain these resources. This will create what is referred to as a **closed ecosystem**, and Azure offers its services in this closed ecosystem for mass consumption. This closed ecosystem allows its consumers to not have to worry about the underlying technology and, in most cases, the operating system needs to support that technology. This has helped in abstracting away the need to support the many facets of technology in today's organizations.

As I grew up in the development world, I had to learn firsthand how frameworks moved the line of responsibility. In the development of applications, this leads to some uncomfortable moments as I had to learn to adjust to these new lines. This learning process allowed me to focus more on the application I was developing and less on how each piece needed to be integrated with the underlying system. New frameworks such as the **Entity Framework** for database integration or the **Windows Identity Framework** for security integration simplified these layers in application development. Azure begins the next evolution of these abstractions and is referred to as a **closed ecosystem**. A closed ecosystem gives the infrastructure resources or operations managers within an organization new lines of responsibility.

These new lines have created an opportunity for organizations to support their daily operations and have put less pressure on underlying infrastructure concerns. This has led to a new way for operational engineers to secure organization resources, which has been simplified and codified. Cloud resources have also stretched passed the need for managing virtual machines alone and have moved to a more utility-based structure (referred to as compute), as you can just deploy your enterprise applications without much regard to the underlying infrastructure. Now, in the past, I have been asked by these operations folks *Why would they want to eliminate my job function?* The simple answer is the same as it was for the developer. It will enhance your ability to complete your job function, and not eliminate it. My answer, personally, when asked this question, is *do you like getting up in the night and on weekends to patch or support your infrastructure?*, to which the answer is always a resounding *No!*, I then ask, *If I could remove this from your view, would that be ok?* This is always answered with a *Yes!*, and I then say, *Welcome to Azure!*

Overall, this is to helped organizations focus on their application development, infrastructure resource needs, and security, without the concern of maintaining, patching, or updating the underlying resources or technology. One of the biggest things organizations have to grasp is the changes to budgeting in this new utility-based cost model. Gone are the days of needing to rent data centers or rack space to house your servers and routers. In their place steps the consumption model. This model follows more of a pay as you go aspect for resources and has opened the door for organizations and startups to better structure budgets and the upfront costs of development or infrastructure. With that comes some caveats, as with electricity, some things you put into this model can create unexpected costs. For example, plugging in a refrigerator or pool pump can increase your monthly bill, and so resources such as CosmosDB or VM sizing can affect your Azure monthly bill. As we progress through this book, we will hopefully bring more of these issues to light and learn how to control costs better.

With the adoption of the cloud, there has come new guidance on the usage of resource types, cost, as well as deployment needs. These needs and deployment strategies differ by a cloud provider, but one I have been very accustomed to us is Azure. Azure provides **Platform as a service (PaaS)**, **Software as a service (SaaS)**, and **Infrastructure as a service (IaaS)** for a large variety of programming languages. One of the biggest hurdles in your journey beside which type of resources to use is the cost associated with spinning up that type of resource. Most of the clients I work with have struggled with cost management. I try to leverage the Azure pricing calculator as much as I can; however, with Azure being a utility, it never tells the tale of consumption. So, as we begin our journey to Azure enlightenment, we will look at the cost or highlighting the things you need to consider when selecting a resource. Let's take a moment to look at the responsibility to understand what responsibilities you are keeping and are releasing Microsoft, in following figure:

	On-prem	IaaS	PaaS	Serverless	SaaS
Physical Security	Client	Microsoft	Microsoft	Microsoft	Microsoft
Host Infrastructure	Client	Microsoft	Microsoft	Microsoft	Microsoft
Operating System	Client	Client	Microsoft	Microsoft	Microsoft
Network Controls	Client	Client	Split	Split	Microsoft
Identity & Access Management	Client	Client	Split	Split	Microsoft
Logistical Application Server	Client	Client	Split	Microsoft	Microsoft
Application Logic	Client	Client	Client	Client	Microsoft
Client Endpoints	Client	Client	Client	Client	Split
Data Classification	Client	Client	Client	Client	Client

Client Owned ☐   Microsoft Owned ▨

Now that we understand the responsible parties on the type of resources we pick, let's dive into Azure and see how to leverage it to run solutions.

Before you start, have a plan

One of the things you want to do before you start your journey is to put a plan or governance together. This will help with keeping everyone honest and set the expectation on what is important to consider when building your solutions. As you can see in the following figure, we look at governance from a design, execute, and review perspective to keep things simple.

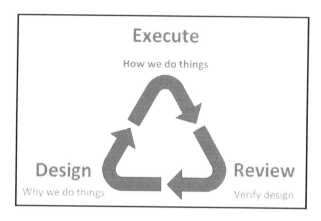

Azure governance approach

This is meant to answer the questions as to "Why we do things", "How we do things", then how we verify and change our governance. The "why" component becomes your vision and constraints such as regulatory obligations, privacy, or data related needs. The "how" component is the required needs like policies, encryption, and so on, which can be implemented and controlled. The "verify" component provides the verification of the implementation of the design, but also, we flexible enough to allow changes based on new innovations in the cloud.

Your journey to the cloud should provide the following key attributes:

- A more personalized and rich experience when engaging your customer
- A fast-moving transformation of products
- Empowering your employees to innovate
- Optimizing your organization through DevOps

Not that we have our plan, let's look at how we get started using Azure.

How do I start using Azure?

When one starts using Azure, there are many new things to learn, like how resources are configured and used in the environment. So, I headed over to the Azure portal (`https://portal.azure.com`) and created an account. There are several things to consider here; you can pay as you go, configure an Enterprise Agreement, use an Azure Pass, sign up for Dev Essentials, or use an MSDN subscription to set up how you will pay for the resources. You can also configure spending limits to help control costs and also control enterprise costs. With an Enterprise Agreement, you can use a Dev/Test subscription to help offset costs. Enterprise Agreement Dev/Test subscriptions get you a significant price reduction, percentage-wise, over production versions. If you plan on using Azure a lot, I would recommend engaging with Microsoft to get an Enterprise Agreement. To get an Enterprise Agreement, you will need to reach out to a Microsoft account representative for the requirements, which you can review here: `https://www.microsoft.com/en-us/licensing/licensing-programs/enterprise.aspx`. As a side note, you can also create your account through Office 365 services, but for the sake of simplification, we will stick with the Azure portal side. Once your account has been created, you will access the portal and be presented with the Azure default dashboard. For a Tenant to be created, you must have what is referred to as a privileged account, which is defined as an Azure account in the Tenant or Enterprise Agreement. At the end of the day, it is an organization's network account.

Once the Tenant has been created, it will act as a virtual representation of your organization within Azure. This equates to the earlier physical network structures that were used within an organization which was secured by firewalls, network resources, and directory services that were usually housed in a data center. A Tenant in Azure follows the same structural basis but is a virtual instance of the organization that is backed by the **Azure Active Directory** (**AAD**) services. All Tenants require AAD, as this is the digital identity service model for securing all SaaS, IaaS, and PaaS resources. Think of the Tenant as your organization container, with the same type of physical boundaries as a physical data center network would have. The following diagram shows a simplified view of a Tenant:

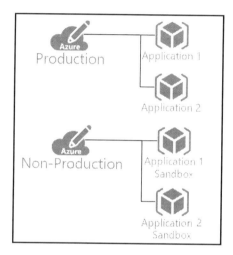

AAD services, as shown in the preceding diagram, can be synchronized with an on-premise **Active Directory** (**AD**) through a process called **Active Directory Federation Service** (**ADFS**). This is the process of *syncing* users/groups and helps with providing access to cloud and on-premises resources without the need to add users to both directory services. Now that we have our Tenant, it has hard resource sharing boundaries that can't be broken, just like your physical network. A Tenant is also assigned a Tenant ID that is used to identify the organization, and the privileged account is assigned the owner. Within your Tenant, you have an Office 365 or O365 container that houses your SaaS products such as Exchange, SharePoint, Power App, and so on, and the Azure Container that houses your subscriptions and resource groups. This book isn't about O365 and the SaaS-based container, but more about the Azure container and the guidance needed to architect, develop and deploy solutions. Now, regarding Azure, we need to discuss the structure of how resources are handled: you start with a Tenant, then you have a subscription, and then you have a resource group, as shown in the following diagram:

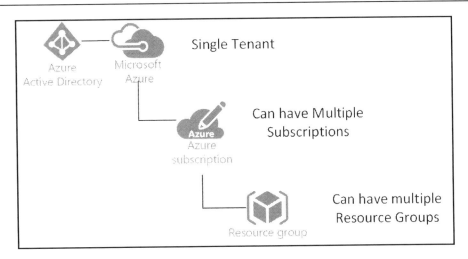

A **Subscription (Sub)** in Azure is a container that groups together resources and users, and also has limits. The limits have changed over time and can be increased with support tickets from Microsoft. You can review the limits at `https://docs.microsoft.com/en-us/azure/azure-subscription-service-limits`. Subs themselves have sharing limits as well. For instance, currently, Key Vaults, App Service Certs, and Express Routes, to name a few, do not span subscriptions. You can also include resources in **Resource Groups (RG)** from another subscription. You also do not have the **intellisense** in the portal for resources, not in the same subscriptions. RGs are application life cycle resource containers within a subscription that houses all the resources that make an application or piece of an application or infrastructure. You create a subscription when your tenant is created. You can also do this through your Enterprise Portal.

Architectural tip:
When you have created your Tenant and start building out your Subs, you should keep to a simplistic approach. This means that you should start minimally, for example, you should have a Tenant and a Sub or two. I generally start with a production Sub and a non-production Sub. In your non-production Sub, you should get Dev/Test pricing through you EA or use MSDN as your non-production Sub by using resource groups at application containers.

The reason for this suggestion is that resources have boundaries, and hybrid solutions require VPNs or Express Route, which have Sub boundaries and require VNet integration to other Subs, which will become multiple points of failure. I suggest you only add more Subs based on very specific needs, such as client work you need to transfer later on to a client.

I have set up my Tenant – what's next?

After you have configured and set up your Tenant and Subs, perform the following steps:

1. Let's login into the portal at `https://portal.azure.com/`. Once you have signed into Azure, you will enter the default dashboard.

    Dashboards are extremely powerful, and we will discuss leveraging them at each step in supporting and monitoring the resources that are built.

2. Now, there are several ways we can add resources through the portal, but in this first section, we will add them into the portal. There are several ways to search for resources using the portal once you have logged in, as shown in the following screenshot:

Resource search on Azure Portal

3. You can use the top search for quick resource lookup by typing in the name of the resource you need, for example, `App Service Cert` or `Certificates`.

4. If you would like to search by visible name, you can use the **All Services** link from the side menu. This will bring up the services blade, as shown in the following screenshot:

All services blade

Now, some resources come from the Azure Marketplace, such as VM images and Web Applications. These are provided from the Marketplace via ARM resource deployments that are created by Microsoft or certified vendors. The **Azure Resource Management (ARM)** are template systems that are used by Azure deployment mechanisms. These are basically JSON files that describe the resources being deployed. We will discuss them in details in Chapter 6, *Deploying Solutions to Azure*. The marketplace is a great starting place for applications such as WordPress.

Let's walk through a marketplace example

Let's walk through an example of how to set up a WordPress site using on the Portal and Marketplace. This will not only provide an understanding of how to use the Marketplace but how the underlying ARM templates are leveraged in the deployment of resources from the Marketplace:

1. In the top search bar, type `Marketplace`, as follows:

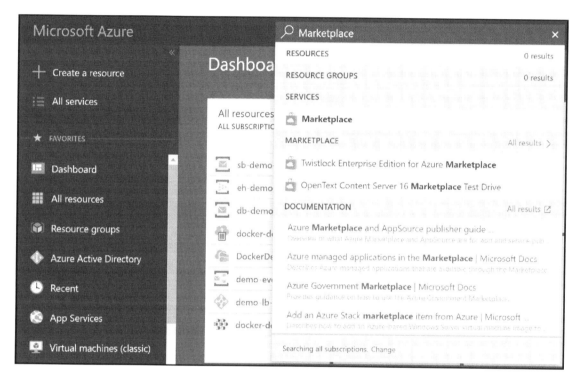

2. Select **Marketplace** from the services menu.

3. Once the **Marketplace** blade is open, select **Everything** and type `WordPress`, as follows:

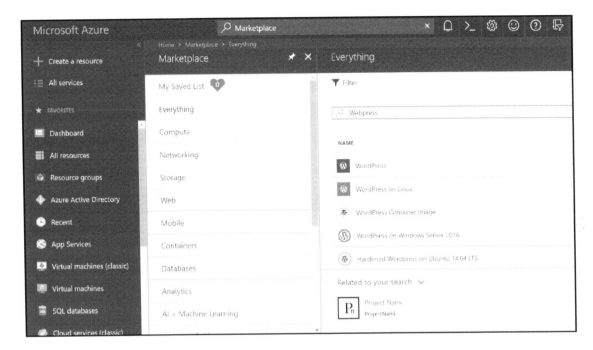

4. Select the first **WordPress** in the list.

5. Click on the **Create** button, as shown in the following screenshot:

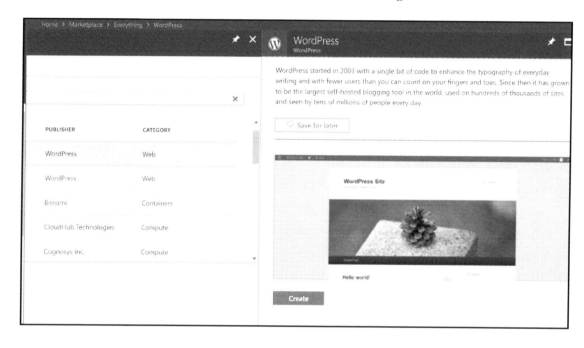

6. Enter an **App Name**, **Subscription**, **Resource Group Name**, and **Database Provider** to **Azure Database for MySQL**. Leave the **App Service plan/Locations** settings as their default options for the demo:

7. For this walk-through, when you click on **Database** and the **Database** blade comes up, just add a password, select a basic pricing tier, and click **OK**:

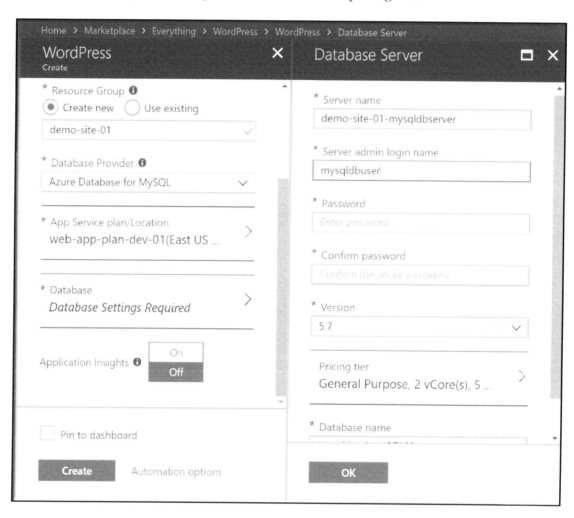

8. Then, click the **Create** button.
9. Once this has been created, you will receive a notification stating that is has been completed. Click on **Go to resource**, where you will be able to access and configure your WordPress site.

   Optional steps to add a custom domain and SSL Certificate

10. Go to your App Service Resource and click on **Custom Domains**, use the IP Address to point your domain at, once you add your A record, then click on + **Add Hostname** to add.

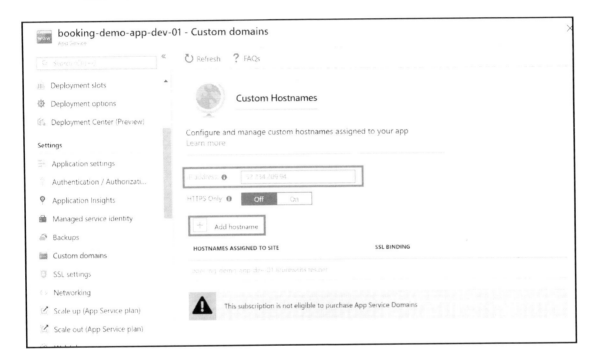

11. You will need to add your private or public certs, which you can leverage App Service Certificates (which I recommend), and once added, **+Add a Binding** and turn on HTTPS only.

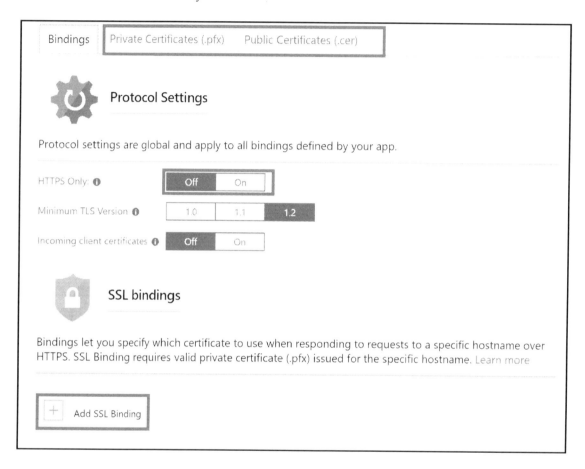

During this exercise, we created several things: an App Service, an App Service Plan, a MySQL server, and a MySQL database instance. An **App Service** is the instance of code needed to run the application. In this case, this is the WordPress PHP code. This is connected to the Marketplace code repository that, in most cases, keeps the code updated based on refreshes to the Marketplace. It is deployed from the Marketplace using a process called ARM template. An **ARM template** is a JSON representation of the resources that are deployed to an Azure Resource Group. The ARM template process leverages a **Desired State Configuration (DSC)**, to manage the configuration state of the resources, and this process helps with creating or updating the resources should the template be run again to update the resources within the application Resource Group. In the case of WordPress, the updates are handled by the portal. An **App Service Plan**, commonly call VM backed, is the virtual resources allocated to the App Service. Think of the VM as something that houses the web server, and the App Service as an IIS app on the box. The **MySQL server** instance houses the MySQL database instance for the WordPress site, which is almost the same as the on-premise version in IIS, but is instance-based and hides the server's implementation. So, as you can see, the implementation of the application is basically the same as it would be on-premise, but it is more instance-based in Azure. There is no need to worry about the infrastructure implementation as you would with an on-premise solution.

The App Service Plan controls the resources used to back up your App Service for dev or demo environments. I would use Free or Shared to help keep the cost down. If you require custom URLs or SSL, you will need to use a basic or standard plan, which will increase the cost significantly, so be mindful of the requirements you need for your App Service. For larger organization you can get premium tiers and for those using PII or GDPR you can leverage isolated tier or App Service Environment or ASE to isolate applications and protect data.

Extending Directory Services to Azure

Organizations have leveraged Directory Services and Identity Services for years, and they have manifested in the Azure Active Directory in Azure. The **Azure Active Directory (AAD)**, is important for securing services for Azure-based solutions. Before we discuss moving existing applications to Azure in Chapter 2, *Moving existing apps to Azure*, it is a good practice to *synchronize* directories so that resources can be shared from on-premise to Azure in hybrid scenarios. A hybrid scenario would be defined as moving your web front-end virtual machines into Azure while your databases' virtual machines remain on-premise. You can leverage Azure Connect to solve the syncing of your on-premise Active Directory to Azure Active Directory, as shown in the following diagram:

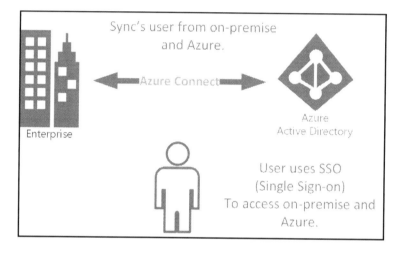

Azure AD Connect

While this book is about *Hands-On Solutions with Azure*, the configuration of the synchronization to Azure can be complex based on the directory services configured within your organization. You can find Azure Connect in the portal, as shown in the following screenshot.

You can also learn how to set up Azure Active Directory to sync with your organization by using the guide at https://docs.microsoft.com/en-us/azure/active-directory/connect/active-directory-aadconnect, as you can see below in Figure 1.7.

Azure Connect in the portal

No matter how you choose to use Azure, it is important to get the security right upfront. Now, one of the biggest differences is that the Azure Active Directory has pricing plans based on the type of services you need, and you can review that pricing here: `https://azure.microsoft.com/en-us/pricing/details/active-directory/`.

> Make sure to move all of your domains first. You want to use OU filtering to ensure that only the people you want are synchronized. Moving resources to a non-sync OU will reduce the object's sync, for example, there may be people that have left or services not in use.

Once everything has been completed, your users should be able to change their passwords on both fronts. You will also have the ability to access and secure resources without having to add them to Azure AD and cut down on your user management.

Terminology to remember with Azure

These words have very specific meanings in Azure, and need to be referenced in the proper context to avoid confusion:

- **Tenant**: This is a representative of an organization. It is a dedicated instance of the Azure Active Directory service that an organization receives and owns when it creates a relationship with Microsoft. This is the top level starting point of your virtual organization in Azure.
- **Subscription**: This groups together users and the resources that have been created by those users. This is the next level of container housing in Azure regarding resources and has limits to the number of resources it can house.
- **Resource Group**: This is simply an identifier that the Azure Resource Manager applies to resources to group them together. This is generally used as an application boundary within Azure and is the application life-cycle container.
- **AAD**: Azure Active Directory or Directory/Identity services for Azure.
- **B2C**: Business to Customer, an implementation of AAD for customers.
- **RBAC**: Role-Based Access Control is a security feature Azure uses to grant access to things like Resource Groups.

Summary

Now that we have created our tenant, subscriptions, and our first resource group using the Marketplace, let's review some key points and terminology. A tenant is the virtual representation and the main container for all of your organization resources in Azure and is Azure Active Directory backed for security and identity management. A subscription is a container that groups resources and users together and has resource limits. You want to take a simplistic approach to create a subscriptions as they have sharing boundaries. Additionally, you want to use resource groups as an application life cycle container to house the resources required for your application. You will want to leverage the marketplace or ARM templates as deployment process for your resources within a resources group, allowing the DSC to manage the state of the resources within the resource group. Use dashboards to view your resource groups in order to monitor and support your deployed resources.

With this new understanding, you might ask, *I have an existing application I would love to move to Azure*. The next part of our journey will look at migrating or leveraging parts of Azure with your existing applications. We will cover everything from *lift and shift* to hybrid solutions, and what it means to host them.

Questions

Let's take a look at what we have learned so far:

1. What is the URL to access the portal?
2. What is an Azure Tenant?
3. What is a subscription?
4. What do you use a Resource Group for?
5. What is an ARM template?
6. What does DSC stand for?
7. What is AAD?

Further reading

These links will be helpful in understanding a few of the topics we have covered in more detail:

- Azure Documentation: https://docs.microsoft.com/en-us/azure/
- Azure Portal: https://portal.azure.com/
- Azure Resource Limits: https://docs.microsoft.com/en-us/azure/azure-subscription-service-limits
- Azure Pricing Calculator: https://azure.microsoft.com/en-us/pricing/calculator/
- Azure Connect: https://docs.microsoft.com/en-us/azure/active-directory/connect/active-directory-aadconnect
- Azure Active Directory Pricing: https://azure.microsoft.com/en-us/pricing/details/active-directory/
- Enterprise Agreement: https://www.microsoft.com/en-us/licensing/licensing-programs/enterprise.aspx

Moving Existing Apps to Azure 2

Now that we have our Azure environment, in this chapter, we will cover what to do next with our existing apps. Should I *lift and shift*, or migrate? How do I build out resources, move existing code, and make cost considerations? Whether you are looking to move your SaaS, IaaS, or PaaS-based solution, you might be able to migrate them to Azure with minimal-to-no code changes, except for application configuration. During this process, we will discuss how to use hybrid models for those legacy applications that aren't good candidates for Azure for third-party or regulatory reasons.

In this chapter, we will cover the following topics:

- Moving apps to Azure
- Building Azure resources
- Deploying existing code to Azure
- How to cost manage your decisions

Technical requirements

The requirements for this chapter are as follows:

- Visual Studio or Visual Studio Code - `https://www.visualstudio.com/`
- Visual Studio Team Services - `https://www.visualstudio.com/team-services/`
- Azure Power Shell - `https://docs.microsoft.com/en-us/powershell/azure/overview?view=azurermps-6.2.0`
- Site-to-Site VPN using PowerShell - `https://docs.microsoft.com/en-us/azure/vpn-gateway/vpn-gateway-create-site-to-site-rm-powershell`
- ExpressRoute - `https://docs.microsoft.com/en-us/azure/expressroute/`
- Exchange Service Deployment Assistant - `https://technet.microsoft.com/en-us/office/dn756393.aspx`

How I approach the discussion

When I begin a discussion on migration to Azure with an organization, it is a bit different than a greenfield discussion because we have something in our hands. We know the size, shape, and history of the application we are moving. Let's look at things we should do in this scenario.

We want to start by assessing the applications and infrastructure, and we do this in the following way:

- Discovery, which allows us to peek under the hood of the applications and infrastructure needed to support them. This is not only the code but such things as DNS and services needed to support the application. This is helpful, as not every application is a good candidate to migrate or you may need to secure VPN connect to the internal resources that can't be moved to Azure.
- This will lead to mapping your applications to discover all dependencies, which to me is the best exercise as every single organization I have consult with discovered something new with this process.
- Once you have all this together, you can evaluate which applications make good candidates to move to Azure and which ones need to be modernized.

Once you have gathered this information, you will have some choices to make and it is good to get into those uncomfortable conversations within the organization so as to fit your applications into one of the following buckets:

- Rehost
- Refactor
- Re-architect
- Rewrite

Let's take a deeper look into what these mean and how each has its own merits depending on the state of your application and discovery.

Rehost

Rehosting is the basic approach to the **lift and shift** model. There are no code changes and it is basically the fastest way to migrate. I just want to remind everyone that this can be the costliest approach to moving to Azure, but is arguably the simplest.

We use this approach in the following situations:

- There is a need to move applications into Azure quickly
- Applications require being run on a VM
- You do not want to change code or can't (no source code)

Once migrated, I will look for opportunities to optimize, but usually in this scenario there aren't many opportunities other than rapid scaling.. Let's look at what this would look like:

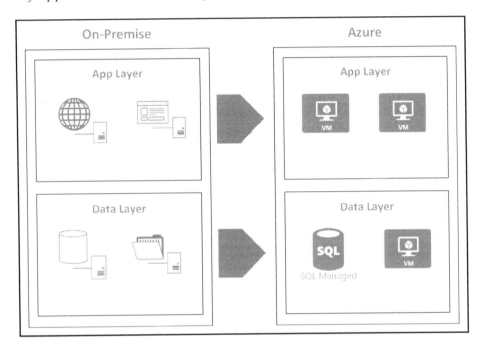

Some good tools to assist in this type of migration are the following:

- **Azure Site Recovery**: `https://azure.microsoft.com/en-us/services/site-recovery/`
- **Data Migration Tool**: `https://azure.microsoft.com/en-us/services/database-migration/`

Now, it is at this point that we need to remember that this type of environment will need boundaries like an on-premise environment does, so don't forget about your firewalls, load balancer, and routing. Quite a few organizations forget about these and then get burned on their budget because of the cost of these resources. With the complexity of on-premise networks, you should list all the resources you will need. Also, keep in mind, that you can use your licenses to help lower the cost of the VM in Azure.

Refactor

Another Azure migration is to **refactor**, which involves making some changes to the application but not wholesale changes that completely change the code base. For instance, instead of moving the VM, only move the web application. This would require some configuration or code changes to make this happen, which we will discuss in depth in this chapter.

When I have done this, I do the following:

- Assess how to quickly modernize the app to leverage Azure better while keeping costs down
- Provide more code portability and code reuse
- Assess when I want a better DevOps and continuous innovation journey

I approach refactoring for Azure in the following way:

- I review the code to ensure that dependencies are able to run in the cloud
- I review data structures that might need to be moved into Azure
- I look for VPN/Express Route opportunities to leverage on-premise resources over wholesale moves.

An example of this was when I had a client that wanted to move their web frontends to Azure without moving the data repositories into Azure. I started the POC with a site-to-site VPN and then transitioned to ExpressRoute. This begins the process of moving in line with your Azure governance/plan process if you choose this process based on the plan. Let's look at this process in the following diagram:

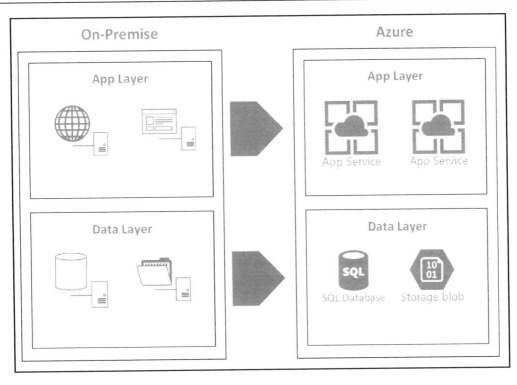

As you can see in the preceding diagram, we did not move the VM but moved the IIS applications to App Services and the data repositories to data instances. This will require us to make changes to the configuration and code updates to interact with these new instance-based services. This allows us to scale differently and control cost a bit better.

Re-architect

Re-architecting is the start of a more intrusive approach to migrating to Azure, as it will require you to modify or extend your code base to align more with modern approaches to scale and optimization. This is a more costly effort in the context of the overall investment if your code base and will require more business sign-off and testing.

I use this approach in the following situations:

- When I need to evolve an application to be Azure compatible.
- When I need an application to scale better and the code not written to scale

Let's take a quick look at how this might look in the following diagram:

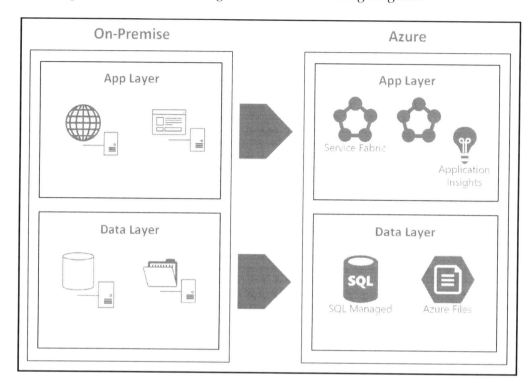

As you can see, re-architecting may change the shape of your application and require some business buy-off to cover resource costs, but, at the end of the day, will help the overall application and its success moving to Azure.

Rewrite

Rewriting is the most intrusive process, as you will be starting from scratch with your application and this by far includes the most business commitment. You will be gathering new requirements and possibly changing the flow of the application because the application is no longer supportable in its current condition.

I use this approach in the following situations:

- When an application is past its lifespan and functionality or relies on outdated third-party resources
- When I need to use more cloud-native technologies

As you can see in the following diagram, the application is completely written to take advantage of new modern resources in Azure:

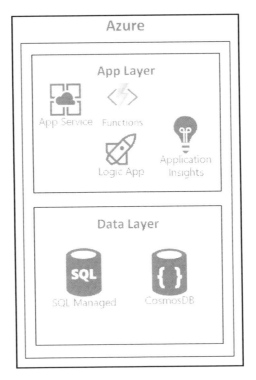

As you can see, the application is leveraging all the new Azure components, but let's look at some simple migrating to Azure.

Creating resources in the Azure Portal

Before we look at using ARM templates, let's review how we create our resources within the portal and we will also see how we can get the automation scripts to help with our ARM templates and PowerShell script. We will walk through creating a VM in Azure with the following steps:

1. Log into the Azure portal (`https://portal.azure.com/`)
2. Once logged in, you can click **+ Create a resource**, select the resource you would like to create, and then fill in the required information.

3. Once it has been created, head over to the resource and scroll down to
Automation script. There you will find your PowerShell and JSON template files
that you can download and include in a Visual Studio project. You will need to
modify the parameters and such, but it's really a great starting place:

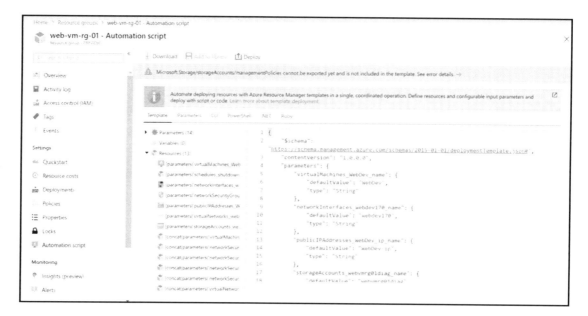

This was helpful to me, as I was able to visualize the code to better understand it. Now let's
move on to the JSON and PowerShell ARM templates.

Migrating to Azure

Now that we have configured our tenant, let's look at some ways to migrate enterprise
systems, VMs, or applications to Azure. While this book is hands-on with solutions in the
cloud, I thought I would take a brief moment to talk about SaaS solutions as they may
become an important part of providing well-rounded solutions in Azure.

Let's talk SaaS migrations

When an organization looks to move to Azure, it's usually not just legacy applications or new greenfield development, but actually, some Enterprise packaged solutions like Exchange, SharePoint, or Dynamics. As we discussed in `Chapter 1`, *Getting Started with Azure*, this all starts with Azure Active Directory. With the complications of systems deployed within organizations, there isn't a one size fits all or a magic bullet for migrating to Azure, so I would like to give you some gotchas and pointers on how to get started with migrating your SaaS solutions in Office 365.

> Before you start, it is a good idea to have an inventory of all your assets, such as sites, site collections, listed libraries, and the size of your databases.

Office 365

Migrating to Office 365 requires planning and a pretty good knowledge of the environment you are going to migrate to. This will help you decide on the type of migration you need, for example, cut-over versus staged or hybrid migration. To help with this, you can use the Exchange Server Deployment Assistant at `https://technet.microsoft.com/en-us/office/dn756393.aspx`.

The aforementioned migration choices can be explained as follows:

- **Cut-over**: This is a one shot and you're done technique regarding moving all your data to Office 365. I would suggest you use the Assistant because there are limits as to how many mailboxes can be moved.
- **Staged**: This is a batch version of cut-over, where you move all your data in stages. This is a more managed approach to migrating.
- **Hybrid**: This option extends an on-premise server, and can be a permanent state or temporary. This option requires Azure AD Connect sync with an on-premise AD.

You will want to use multi-factor authentication, DLP anti-spam, encryption, and rights management, especially in the healthcare or financial arena. Migrations do not handle server-side public folders, archive data, or emails larger than 25 MB, nor client-side PST or local settings. This can make things tricky, especially in hybrid scenarios.

Migration uses a lot of bandwidth, to ensure that you have the right circuit assigned or pick a time off hours. Also, deleted emails, by default, are saved for 14 days. You can increase this to 30 days by changing the Messaging Recording Management policy.

Looking at the solutions such as Dynamics and SharePoint, it is important to know that on-premise is most likely a version behind the cloud version and that most on-premise solutions work in Azure, but you must remember to test them.

SharePoint Farm level solutions are not supported in SharePoint online, so if your on-premise environment uses them, then you will need to rewrite them.

Let's talk IaaS

When looking at migrating an existing application to Azure, most people fall back on what they know, which is to move the virtual machines or use the **lift and shift** model. While lift and shift appear to be the easiest way to move your legacy application in the least cost-effective way, this can be very useful and fast when moving legacy applications to Azure that have not been modernized or have dependencies on third-party resources that may not have been modernized as well. With on-premise Active Directory services being synchronized with Azure Active Directory, help and virtual machine management are provided through an already established process, helping you ease into the Azure model. This means that the virtual machine and services you move to Azure can still leverage their service accounts to function, as well as the data access service accounts, to your databases. Databases and AD services can also be moved out as managed services, meaning you can use domain joining within Active Directory domain services and move existing SQL databases as they are. This can be used to help bridge gaps when modernizing your applications.

Virtual machines in Azure are part of the IaaS. This would also refer to the infrastructure needed to support the virtual machines, like firewalls, gateways, routers, and so on. These will still need to be managed in a traditional way, such as patching.

A hybrid setup for sharing services generally requires a permanent connection to Azure, like a **Virtual Private Network (VPN)** or Express route, so as to expose the internal corporate network to Azure securely. At the beginning of this chapter, links were provided to configure a VPN or ExpressRoute to Azure. Because of network complications and devices, I would suggest you use the links for these configurations.

When considering using a VPN or Express Route solution for your hybrid solution, there are some things to note. First, Express Routes are bound to a subscription, so keeping a simplified subscription model helps with not having to manage too many VNET to VNET connections. Second, it leverages dynamic routing and does not support static routing.

The following diagram shows moving virtual machines into Azure and leveraging a VPN/Express Route to access on-premise services, as you can see:

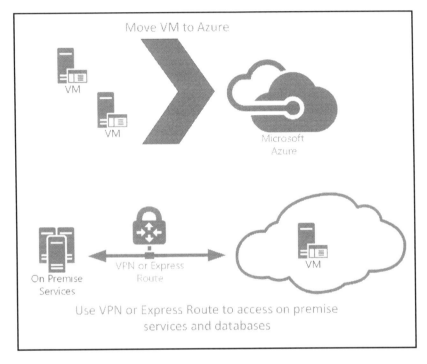

Simple VM move and on-premise services access

As we discussed in the previous chapter, Azure resources are deployed via ARM templates using PowerShell or Azure DevOps deployment services to deploy the resources. ARM templates allow you to create, update, or delete all resources within the template. The templates use a parameters file that can be used to point at different environments and use a declarative syntax to define what resources are getting deployed, as we will see in a moment. Let's save the Azure DevOps version for our deployment chapter and focus on the PowerShell version. Let's discuss this structure before I show you a script that I use to deploy a virtual machine, which is modified from the standard one.

PowerShell and ARM Template

Before we get started on this section, make sure that you have installed the Azure Development Workload, as shown in the following screenshot:

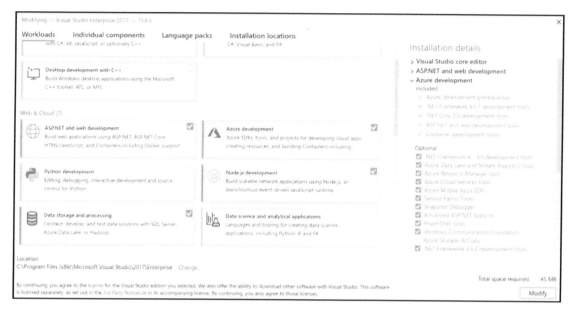

Azure Development Workload in Visual Studio

Let's take a look at the basic structure of the template system used to deploy resources to Azure:

```
{
  "$schema":
"http://schema.management.azure.com/schemas/2015-01-01/deploymentTemplate.j
son#", "contentVersion": "",
  "parameters": { },
  "variables": { },
  "functions": { },
  "resources": [ ],
  "outputs": { }
}
```

Let's look at what the elements in the schema mean and whether some of them are required:

$schema	JSON Schema location	Is required
contentVersion	Your version value to track versions (1.0.0.0)	Is required
parameters	Values that are provided during deployment from a parameters file or Parameters in the Azure DevOps deployment pipeline	Not required
variables	Common values provided as JSON fragments	Not required
functions	User-defined functions	Not required
resources	Type of resources being deployed	Is required
outputs	Return values	Not required

Now that we have seen how the template is structured, let's look at how a vanilla virtual machine is deployed to put it all together. You can create an ARM template project in Visual Studio by selecting the **Azure Resource Group** project under **New Projects**, as shown in the following screenshot:

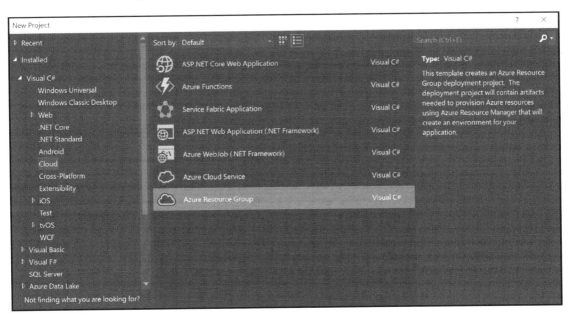

Visual Studio – Azure Resource Group

Deploy-AzureResourceGroup.ps1

In this PowerShell script, we are going to check to see if you are logged in. If you are not logged in, the script will run a validation on your script, create a storage area, upload files to the storage, assign a 4-hour access key, and then run the deployment. The majority of PowerShell is generated when you select an Azure Resource Manager in Visual Studio, but I did add the following login function to help ensure that I am logged in to the right tenant:

```
function Check-Login
{
    $needLogin = $true
    Try
    {
        $content = Get-AzureRmContext
        if ($content)
        {
            $needLogin = ([string]::IsNullOrEmpty($content.Account))
        }
    }
    Catch
    {
        if ($_ -like "*Login-AzureRmAccount to login*")
        {
            $needLogin = $true
        }
        else
        {
            throw
        }
    }
    if ($needLogin)
    {
        Login-AzureRmAccount
    }
}
Check-Login
```

azuredeploy.parameters.json

This file contains the parameters for the template and is called from within the preceding PowerShell script. These parameters will overwrite the parameters in the `Template` file. You can use multiple parameter files to deploy to different environments; I usually also create a different PowerShell file as well by environment so I do not need modify it. I add the parameters for username and password, as well as the private Subnet definition:

```json
{
  "$schema":
"http://schema.management.azure.com/schemas/2015-01-01/deploymentParameters
.json#",
  "contentVersion": "1.0.0.0",
  "parameters": {
    "adminUsername": {
      "value": "azureuser"
    },
    "adminPassword": {
      "value": "Azure12345678"
    },
    "PrivateSubnet": {
      "value": "10.0.1.0/24"
    }
  }
}
```

azuredeploy.json

This is the file that contains the code version of the VM being deployed. It is made up of parameters, which are provided or overwritten by the preceding parameters file. The JSON defines three resources: a VNET, a VM, and a NIC resource. Let's look at how the resources in this file are added and how the sections are broken down. To add resources, you just need to right-click on the resource element in Visual Studio, as you can see in the following screenshot:

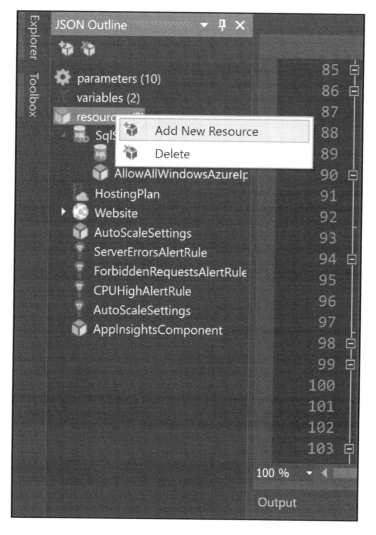

Adding a resource to an ARM Template in Visual Studio

The `parameters` are the input to the template and are the values that are provided by the `parameters` file:

> It is a good practice to provide a meaningful description. Default values can also be provided if they are optional values.

Let's take a look at the following code:

```
{
  "$schema":
"https://schema.management.azure.com/schemas/2015-01-01/deploymentTemplate.
json#",
  "contentVersion": "1.0.0.0",
  "parameters": {
    "adminUsername": {
      "type": "string",
      "metadata": {
        "description": "The name of the administrator account of the new VM
and domain"
      }
    },
    "adminPassword": {
      "type": "securestring",
      "metadata": {
        "description": "The password for the administrator account of the
new VM and domain"
      }
    },
    "PrivateSubnet": {
      "type": "string",
      "defaultValue": "10.0.1.0/24",
      "metadata": { "description": "Private VNet IP Subnet" }
    }
  },
```

The `variables` section is for variables within the template that can leverage functions. As you can see, in the following code, we are using the split function to break apart the `PrivateSubnet` to help create unique names for our VMs:

```
"variables": {
    "GroupStart": "[split(parameters('PrivateSubnet'), '.')[0]]",
    "GroupMain": "[split(parameters('PrivateSubnet'), '.')[1]]",
    "GroupNumber": "[split(parameters('PrivateSubnet'), '.')[2]]",
    "instWin1": "[concat(variables('GroupMain'),'-
',variables('GroupNumber'),'-Win1')]",
```

```
    "instWin1NIC": "[concat(variables('GroupMain'),'-
',variables('GroupNumber'),'-Win1NIC')]",
    "NetworkVNetID": "[resourceId('Microsoft.Network/virtualNetworks',
'NetworkVNet')]",
    "PrivateSubnetName": "PrivateSubnet",
    "PrivateSubnetRef": "[concat(variables('NetworkVNetID'), '/subnets/',
variables('PrivateSubnetName'))]"
  },
```

In the resources section, we define the resource the template will deploy. In this scenario, we are deploying VNet, NIC, and VM resources. The VM will use the NIC card to connect to the VNet. The VNet is the virtual network that the VM will use to communicate to other resources deployed on the VNet. The following code explains how the NIC card is built into the ARM template:

```
    "resources": [
      {
        "apiVersion": "2016-03-30",
        "type": "Microsoft.Network/networkInterfaces",
        "name": "[variables('instWin1NIC')]",
        "location": "[resourceGroup().location]",
        "dependsOn": [
          "[resourceId('Microsoft.Network/virtualNetworks', 'NetworkVNet')]"
        ],
        "properties": {
          "ipConfigurations": [
            {
              "name": "ipconfig1",
              "properties": {
                "privateIPAllocationMethod": "Static",
                "privateIPAddress":
"[concat(variables('GroupStart'),'.',variables('GroupMain'),'.',variables('
GroupNumber'),'.31')]",
                "subnet": {
                  "id": "[variables('PrivateSubnetRef')]"
                }
              }
            }
          ]
        }
      }
```

Now, let's look at VM resource creation and how we add the NIC resource we created previously to the VM. As you can see, in the following code, the NIC is applied as the network interface resource for the VM:

```
{
    "apiVersion": "2016-04-30-preview",
    "type": "Microsoft.Compute/virtualMachines",
    "name": "[variables('instWin1')]",
    "location": "[resourceGroup().location]",
    "dependsOn": [
      "[resourceId('Microsoft.Network/networkInterfaces/',
variables('instWin1NIC'))]"
    ],
    "properties": {
      "hardwareProfile": { "vmSize": "Standard_DS1" },
      "osProfile": {
        "computerName": "[variables('instWin1')]",
        "adminUsername": "[parameters('adminUsername')]",
        "adminPassword": "[parameters('adminPassword')]"
      },
      "storageProfile": {
        "imageReference": {
          "publisher": "MicrosoftWindowsServer",
          "offer": "WindowsServer",
          "sku": "2012-R2-Datacenter",
          "version": "latest"
        },
        "osDisk": {
          "createOption": "FromImage",
          "caching": "ReadWrite"
        }
      },
      "networkProfile": {
        "networkInterfaces": [
          {
            "id":
"[resourceId('Microsoft.Network/networkInterfaces',variables('instWin1NIC')
)]"
          }
        ]
      }
    }
  }
]
}
```

As you can see, the ARM template helps us create a repeatable and configurable process. However, let's look at taking things a bit further. One of the biggest things folks realize is that there are other resources like firewalls, routers, and load balancers that are required when you choose to manage your applications in virtual machines. While this may be a choice that you may not be able to avoid, it also requires you to update the OS and Service Packs.

Let's talk PaaS

When looking at migrating to Azure, sometimes, you need to look past moving the virtual machine to Azure, as you can just move the service itself. Because we are looking at migration and not wholesale code changes, let's pick on some low hanging fruit. In most organizations, you have web applications that usually have databases like SQL to support them. So, for this exercise, let's say that we have virtual machines we want to move—one has two websites and the other has two SQL databases. Instead of moving the two virtual machines, you could just move the websites and databases to Azure as instances. The websites would be deployed to App Services, which is Azure's "IIS" for hosting web applications. Databases would either be migrated to a database instance within an Azure Server resource or through managed instances, which is used to maintain a prior or specific version of SQL. We will dive deeper into this within the next chapter, as well as discuss cost, just looking to start building a quick virtual machine based on understanding. Let's look at how this changes the ARM template. Because the PowerShell is generic, we are not going to review that one again.

Deploy-Azure-WebsiteAndDatabase.parameters.json

In our `parameters` file, we provide the hosting plan name and a username and password for the SQL instance:

```
{
  "$schema":
"https://schema.management.azure.com/schemas/2015-01-01/deploymentParameter
s.json#",
  "contentVersion": "1.0.0.0",
  "parameters": {
    "hostingPlanName": {
      "value": "Demo_Hosting_Plan"
    },
    "administratorLogin": {
      "value": "sqlAdmin"
    },
    "databaseName": {
```

```
    "value": "Pas@word123"
    }
  }
}
```

Deploy-Azure-WebsiteAndDatabase.template.json

The parameters section is the same as the previous section—it is the input to the template. One minor change is the use of the allowed values element, which helps the DSC to complain before the template is executed in the verification process. Let's look at some of the differences between these sections. We won't review the variables section in our discussion:

```
{
  "$schema":
"https://schema.management.azure.com/schemas/2015-01-01/deploymentTemplate.json#",
  "contentVersion": "1.0.0.0",
  "parameters": {
    "hostingPlanName": {
      "type": "string",
      "minLength": 1
    },
    "skuName": {
      "type": "string",
      "defaultValue": "F1"
    },
    "skuCapacity": {
      "type": "int",
      "defaultValue": 1,
      "minValue": 1
    },
    "administratorLogin": {
      "type": "string"
    },
    "administratorLoginPassword": {
      "type": "securestring"
    },
    "databaseName": {
      "type": "string"
    },
    "collation": {
      "type": "string",
      "defaultValue": "SQL_Latin1_General_CP1_CI_AS"
    },
    "edition": {
```

```
        "type": "string",
        "defaultValue": "Basic",
      },
      "maxSizeBytes": {
        "type": "string",
        "defaultValue": "1073741824"
      },
      "requestedServiceObjectiveName": {
        "type": "string",
        "defaultValue": "Basic"
      }
    },
```

Let's see how the SQL instance is deployed within our template. An important thing to note is that the default firewall rules open the SQL instance to all public IP addresses. You will want to tighten the rules for QA and production:

```
  {
      "name": "[variables('sqlserverName')]",
      "type": "Microsoft.Sql/servers",
      "location": "[resourceGroup().location]",
      "tags": {
        "displayName": "SqlServer"
      },
      "apiVersion": "2014-04-01-preview",
      "properties": {
        "administratorLogin": "[parameters('administratorLogin')]",
        "administratorLoginPassword":
  "[parameters('administratorLoginPassword')]"
      },
      "resources": [
        {
          "name": "[parameters('databaseName')]",
          "type": "databases",
          "location": "[resourceGroup().location]",
          "tags": {
            "displayName": "Database"
          },
          "apiVersion": "2014-04-01-preview",
          "dependsOn": [
            "[resourceId('Microsoft.Sql/servers/',
  variables('sqlserverName'))]"
          ],
          "properties": {
            "edition": "[parameters('edition')]",
            "collation": "[parameters('collation')]",
            "maxSizeBytes": "[parameters('maxSizeBytes')]",
            "requestedServiceObjectiveName":
```

```
    "[parameters('requestedServiceObjectiveName')]"
          }
      },
      {
        "type": "firewallrules",
        "apiVersion": "2014-04-01-preview",
        "dependsOn": [
          "[resourceId('Microsoft.Sql/servers/',
variables('sqlserverName'))]"
        ],
        "location": "[resourceGroup().location]",
        "name": "AllowAllWindowsAzureIps",
        "properties": {
          "endIpAddress": "0.0.0.0",
          "startIpAddress": "0.0.0.0"
        }
      }
    ]
  }
```

Now, before we deploy the App Service, we need to have an App Service plan. Let's look at what that element looks like:

```
  {
      "apiVersion": "2015-08-01",
      "name": "[parameters('hostingPlanName')]",
      "type": "Microsoft.Web/serverfarms",
      "location": "[resourceGroup().location]",
      "tags": {
        "displayName": "HostingPlan"
      },
      "sku": {
        "name": "[parameters('skuName')]",
        "capacity": "[parameters('skuCapacity')]"
      },
      "properties": {
        "name": "[parameters('hostingPlanName')]"
      }
  }
```

Now that we have the plan, let's deploy the App Service. An important thing to note is that the connection string to the database is being added to the connections collection in the App Settings of the App Service:

```
  {
      "apiVersion": "2015-08-01",
      "name": "[variables('webSiteName')]",
      "type": "Microsoft.Web/sites",
```

```
      "location": "[resourceGroup().location]",
      "dependsOn": [
        "[resourceId('Microsoft.Web/serverFarms/',
parameters('hostingPlanName'))]"
      ],
      "tags": {
        "[concat('hidden-related:', resourceGroup().id,
'/providers/Microsoft.Web/serverfarms/', parameters('hostingPlanName'))]":
"empty",
        "displayName": "Website"
      },
      "properties": {
        "name": "[variables('webSiteName')]",
        "serverFarmId": "[resourceId('Microsoft.Web/serverfarms',
parameters('hostingPlanName'))]"
      },
      "resources": [
        {
          "apiVersion": "2015-08-01",
          "type": "config",
          "name": "connectionstrings",
          "dependsOn": [
            "[resourceId('Microsoft.Web/Sites/',
variables('webSiteName'))]"
          ],
          "properties": {
            "DefaultConnection": {
              "value": "[concat('Data Source=tcp:',
reference(resourceId('Microsoft.Sql/servers/',
variables('sqlserverName'))).fullyQualifiedDomainName, ',1433;Initial
Catalog=', parameters('databaseName'), ';User Id=',
parameters('administratorLogin'), '@', variables('sqlserverName'),
';Password=', parameters('administratorLoginPassword'), ';')]",
              "type": "SQLServer"
            }
          }
        }
      ]
    }
```

As you can see, this template deployed an App Service Plan, an App Service, and a SQL database. One thing we need to remember is that most resources require infrastructure in order to run, and PaaS resources are no different. App Service Plans, or commonly referred to as VM backed, are the physical resources assigned to run an App Service or a group of App Services. You can think of these as your VM running IIS resources on your virtual machine, which would contain the website code that was deployed to that IIS website. Basically, it is like just moving the website code instead of the entire virtual machine containing IIS. Not only is this more cost-effective in that you no longer have the virtual machine or the infrastructure to support, which costs a lot, but this also allows you to concentrate on application support and remove most of the worry around patching the underlying resources needed to support the website. The SQL database functions in almost the same way as App Services—you create a SQL server instance and then add SQL database instances that use **Data Transfer Units** (**DTU**), which are the VM style resources assigned to run the database instance.

 This is referred to as PaaS, in which you run the instance of the resource in Azure and not the full virtual machine. An example of this would be a web application on a virtual machine that becomes an App Service in Azure without the cost of running the full virtual machine.

The following diagram shows you a simplified view of this process of moving only the instances out to Azure, as you can see in the following diagram:

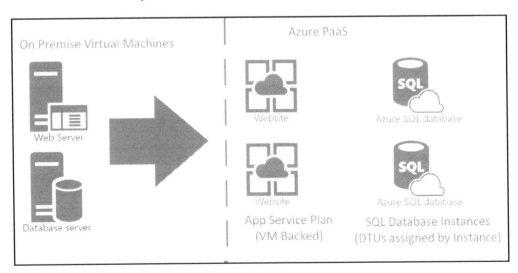

PaaS model

If you need to leverage a custom URL or SSL within an App Service you are going to use, use a Basic or Standard level App Service Plan. For Dev and QA, you can get away with the standard `azurewebsite.net` domain as it has a secure layer to force `https`.

In our `Chapter 3`, *What it takes to Build Solutions in Azure*, we will discuss App Service settings in more detail, however it is worth pointing out now that you can lock down an App Service using the Azure Active Directory service we set up previously with no need to code change. You would want to do this is you have network boundaries that isolate your websites. Once you move it to the cloud, you want to restrict access without having to rewrite the code. You can do this through the App Service with the Azure Portal, as shown in the following screenshot:

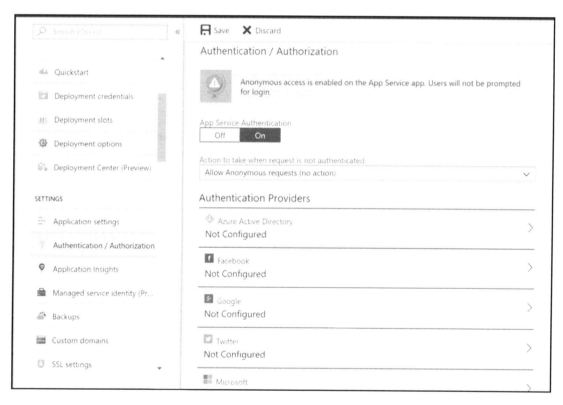

Authentication/Authorization for App Service

Moving legacy applications to Azure can be a tricky thing at the end of the day, but sometimes you have to look past the easy in order to conserve money.

Summary

In this chapter, we have taken a look at what we do with migrating existing legacy applications after we have configured Azure. We also looked at the ARM template and how we deploy resources, as well as at shared resources between on-premise and Azure. We discussed using Azure Connect to sync on-premise AD to Azure AD to help with the hybrid model. We also looked at the difference between the IaaS virtual machine and PaaS instance, or container moves to Azure.

Now that we have looked at how to migrate legacy applications to Azure either with **lift and shift** or instance base, it is time to discuss how we architect solutions within Azure.

Questions

Let's take a look at what we have learned in this chapter:

1. What does it mean to lift and shift?
2. What is an Azure AD Connect?
3. What does ARM stand for?
4. Can templates be used for multiple environments?
5. What is another name for the App Service Plan?
6. What are DTUs?
7. What is IaaS?
8. What is PaaS?

Further reading

Azure documentation can be found here: https://docs.microsoft.com/en-us/azure/

Building Solutions in Azure 3

Now that we have taken a look at how to approach migrating your existing application to Azure, it is time to discuss how to approach building new applications in Azure. This starts with an understanding of the resources involved and when/how to leverage IaaS, SaaS, and PaaS in your solutions. We will also cover when you need to pivot your design when the project changes, and how these effects change the underlying approach to the resources being used.

In this chapter, we will cover the following topics:

- How to pick the right resource to develop solutions in Azure
- How to architect solutions in the Azure closed ecosystem
- Things you need to trust when writing applications in Azure

Technical requirements

The requirements for this chapter are as follows:

- Azure Architecture Guide: `https://docs.microsoft.com/en-us/azure/architecture/guide/`
- Azure Naming Convention Guide: `https://docs.microsoft.com/en-us/azure/architecture/best-practices/naming-conventions`
- DTU Calculator: `http://dtucalculator.azurewebsites.net/`

Let me Azure you of something!

As we briefly discussed in Chapter 1, *Getting Started with Azure,* your architecture begins with the subscriptions structure and an overall naming convention. The reason I bring this up is that these go hand in hand from a fundamental perspective. I have learned that there are two paths you can take with respect to your Azure configuration: the corporate path and the consultant path. The corporate path is for organizations that develop their own solutions, and all work is strictly for the organization alone. The consultant path is for those that do work for others and themselves. The reason this becomes important to point out is that this not only affects the structure of your subscriptions, but how the optional parts of the naming convention work.

Now, I like to take a simplistic approach to building things in Azure and when I am architecting solutions in Azure.

Let's take a look at what I mean. When you are building out a subscription model and a naming convention for an organization, you should take a simple approach. One mistake I have found that most people make is that they approach it from an old-school point of view, meaning that they create subscriptions and subsequently their naming conventions in a complicated n-tier or functional perspective, which creates a highly complicated support model. When you are working within an organization, you need to consider what your interaction with Azure will be the same as using Wildcard certificates or Express Route. This is because there are quite a few things in Azure that don't span subscriptions or can span with some help.

However, this creates more complications. There are two schools of thought on organization setups: one is breaking up subscriptions based on departments, and the other is by environments. Some organizations try to blend these concepts together, which can further complicate your Azure environment. I believe a simpler approach to these is beneficial to most organizations, but some would say that resource limits could be hit. However, they can increase either through time (Microsoft increasing the limits) or through support from Microsoft increasing limits via a support ticket. The simplistic environmental approach I take is prod and non-prod. I do this so that I can get Dev/Test pricing for my non-prod environments. I then use resource groups as my application lifecycle containers. I do this for cost saving, as when I use Express Route, I only have to manage VNet peering. This doesn't solve Wildcard Cert issues or other sharing problems, but it simplifies the support for them. Now, for many large organizations, it may make sense to break up subscriptions and your naming convention to include departments as well as prod and non-prod environments.

Let's take a quick look at a simplified view of resource naming based on the naming convention recommendations by Microsoft that can be found at `https://docs.microsoft.com/en-us/azure/architecture/best-practices/naming-conventions`:

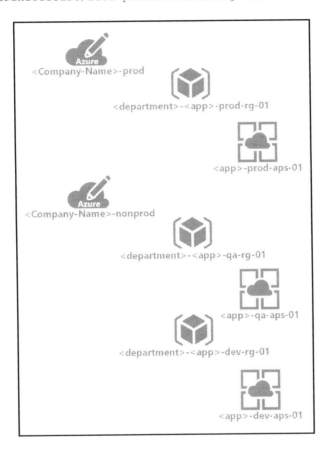

Simplified resource naming

For larger organizations, this would change slightly, but the increase in subscriptions will increase sharing support. Let's see what this looks like. This will create a subscription by department, as well as a prod and non-prod subscription. As you can see, this will complicate your overall Azure, but may be needed for defining boundaries within a large organization:

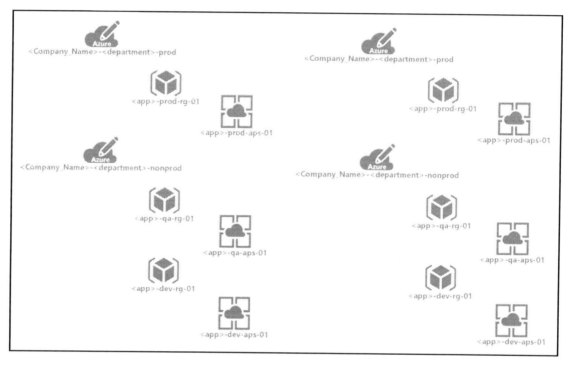

Simplified department resource naming

The naming convention can really be leveraged any way that makes sense to you. I chose this way because it helps in using the search bar to find resources quickly and easily.

Developing a good naming convention is always a good practice within an organization, but develop one that fits you and use the recommendations as guidance during that journey, as this isn't easily changeable in the future without redeploying and migrating.

Now, the change when looking at this from a consultant point of view is to put your clients in their own subscription, which you will mostly do from a prod and non-prod perspective. This is important to remember because subscriptions can be transferred to another tenant, or in some cases, you will create a tenant for them and follow the organizational model. Let's see what these changes will look like:

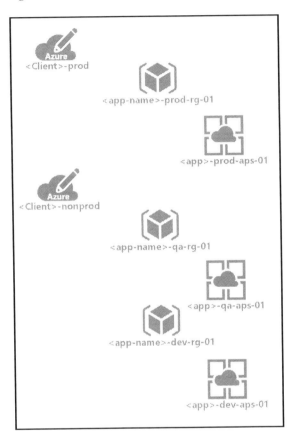

Client simplified resource naming

Now that we have discussed the importance of naming, I would like to point some other important things, such as using **Tags** to identify resources that can be searched or grouped. You can also leverage them to track the finance of a resource or group of resources. I leverage tags to group resources and expose the cost burn on dashboards. These things are architectural in nature but important to know, in order to get specific information from both the portal and PowerShell. First, you want to know how you get tenant information, as well as the subscriptions you have access to. This information is by tenant, which means you will need to switch to the tenant before the information will be available. Once you log in to the Azure portal (`https://portal.azure.com`), you will see your name and an icon in the upper-right-hand part of the portal. You click on the Help (**?**) icon and you will see a link for **Show diagnostics**. This will open your tenant JSON file with all of your information, as you can see in the following screenshot:

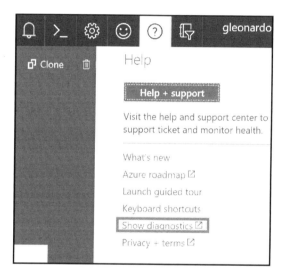

Show diagnostics

Once you click on this link, it will save your tenant JSON file and allow you to open it. I am familiar with this, as I refer to this file a lot in my Azure work. You can also get your TenantID from your AAD property blade, as well as the Directory ID property. You can also get it from using the following command to log in to Azure:

 Always run your PowerShell Console or IDE in administrator mode so that you don't run into permission issues. You can do this by right-clicking on the icon and choosing **Run as Administrator**.

```
Login-azaccount
```

This is the result you should see:

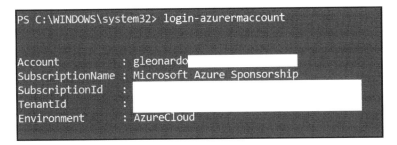

Azure login for PowerShell

You can also get subscription information by running the following command after you run the login script. Your login will carry the whole PowerShell session, so be careful and ensure that you are logged in to the right tenant:

```
get-azurermsubscription
```

This is the result you should see:

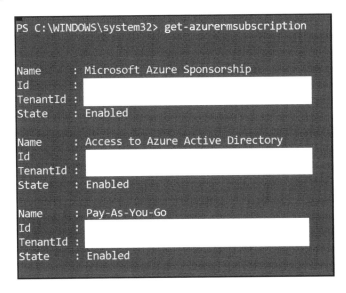

Azure subscription in PowerShell

Azure blueprints

Azure blueprints is something that was added to Azure that allows architects to sketch out the design parameters for a project, which adhere to patterns, standards, and requirement within an organization. The thing that was missing since the beginning was a declarative way to orchestrate the deployment of multiple ARM templates and artifacts, such as:

- Policy assignments
- Role assignments
- ARM templates
- Resource groups

Now one of the things I had to learn was how blueprints differed from ARM templates, which for me, was ARM templates on steroids, meaning not only can you have a set of resource groups, but also roles and policy assignments.

- Life of a blueprint, either through the Azure portal or REST API (I use PowerShell)
- Create and edit; this functions is in draft mode and is not assigned
- Publish, once publish is assigned, it can't be changed
- Create and edit new versions; to change a blueprint you create a new version
- Publish new version; once published, a version can't be changed
- Delete a version (if needed); remove a version
- Delete a blueprint; remove a blueprint

Blueprints can have many version that can be assigned to multiple subscriptions. This can be for an environment set up with different roles or different types of application modules. You also cannot remove a blueprint that is actively assigned to a subscription.

Blueprints, like ARM templates, allow for both static or dynamic input and output parameters. The blueprint, because it is an orchestrator artifact, requires a sequence for deployment and, by default, follows the following sequence by subscription level, as resource group artifacts are sorted by placeholder name:

- Role assignment artifacts by artifact name
- Policy assignment artifacts by artifact name
- ARM template by artifact name

This same process is followed for child resources within each resource group artifact being processed. Now, you can customize the sequence by using the standard dependsOn property with JSON. To gain a deeper understanding, head over to `https://docs.microsoft.com/en-us/azure/governance/blueprints/`. Now it is time to review the responsibility matrix so that we understand what our architecture should be responsible for.

Key Vault

Key Vault was designed as a tool to store keys and secrets, which helps you control access to the vault. It can be used by anyone who has an Azure subscription and have subscription boundaries. Azure Key Vault is also a service that lets you easily provision, manage, and deploy public and private **Secure Sockets Layer/Transport Layer Security (SSL/TLS)** certificates for use with Azure and your internal connected resources.

I work with Key Vault to help with the following:

- **Key management**: To store my keys like encryption keys for securing my data
- **Secret management**: To store my tokens, certificates, API Keys, passwords, and other secrets.

There are three ways to authenticate to Key Vault:

- Use managed identities for Azure resources, which is the recommended approach, as the secrets are rotated automatically
- Use a services principle and certificate, which requires the owner to rotate the certificate rather than being automatic like identities for Azure resources
- Use a service principle and secret, which is the most basic approach to accessing the vault

To create a Key Vault, you can either be in the Azure portal or go through PowerShell. I prefer PowerShell because of its reuse. Let's see how that is done:

```
New-azKeyVault –VaultName 'BookDemo-KeyVault' –ResourceGroupName 'keyvault-prod-rg-01' –Location 'East US'
```

Now, let's add a secret to the vault, again using PowerShell:

```
$secretvalue = ConvertTo-SecureString 'Pass@word1' –AsPlainText –Force
$secret = Set-AzureKeyVaultSecret –VaultName 'BookDemo-KeyVault' –Name 'DemoPassword' –SecretValue $secretvalue
```

One of the biggest examples of usage in Azure is if you use App Services, as I leverage App Services Certificates, which secure App Services and I don't need to remember to rotate them, as Azure does that for me.

Let's look at pricing for Key Vault:

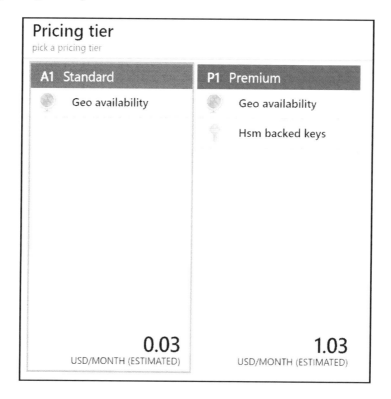

VNet

When you have an internal network, you usually care about the network you plug your resources into. In Azure, that piece is abstracted out of your view in most scenarios. However, you might need to control how your resources interact or you may need to connect your own network to Azure.

I like to use VNet for the following reasons:

- Isolation and segmentation
- Communication between Azure resources

- Communication with o-premise resources
- Filtering network traffic
- Routing network traffic, using routing tables to move traffic between subnets and networks on-premise or via the internet
- Connecting virtual networks in different regions

Let's take a quick look at a simplified VNet implementation that has a public frontend and a private backend:

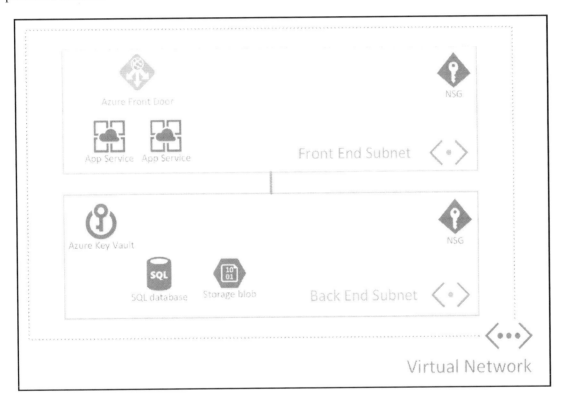

As you can see, we are using a **Network Security Group** (**NSG**), to apply policies to the subnets. One of the policies on the backend subnet is limiting access to the internet. We have an Azure front door service running in front of our app services to provide load balancing and SSL off-loading. In our backend subnet, we are using Key Vault to store our secrets and keys. This is just a simple way to show how to use a VNet in Azure.

Mobile

Azure can assist with mobile development for using Azure AD or Azure B2C to secure your app so as to use CosmosDB to store telemetry. Mobile apps generally rely on services within the cloud to provide or store data. One of the biggest things I like is that you can use these services in Xamarin. This allows you to create a native app all from a single code base written in C#. So, to quickly summarize, mobile apps can provide the following:

- Authentication and authorization, through directory services or OAuth services
- Data access
- Offline sync
- Push notification

Mobile apps function like App Services and while native device development isn't truly about Azure, I wanted to make note that mobile development will be one of the cornerstone services provided by Azure. So, I would recommend that you get your team up to speed with Xamarin development so you can rapidly provide mobile solutions when needed. This is how I would approach a mobile app in Azure, with my team using Xamarin to do the development:

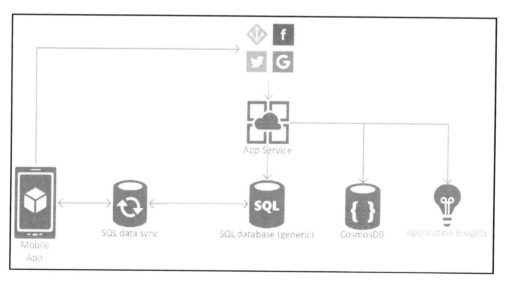

As you can see, I would use a social account, Azure B2C, or both to secure my app, plan for offline syncing (if data is important), while leveraging an app/mobile service with SQL and/or CosmosDB as the data repository. Application Insight would be my error log, to not only trap my application errors but also my service-based errors.

IoT

IoT devices, such as mobile devices, have a similar flow in Azure, as generally, the backend services are consumed by the IoT device. There are a few caveats. IoT devices have two specialized elements in Azure; one is the IoT hub, which is an implementation of an event hub but targets IoT, and IoT Central. Let's look at how we can use IoT Central to discover an IoT story for an organization.

Head to `https://apps.azureiotcentral.com/` and log in. Once there, create an app:

Click the + sign and then enter the application info. I like to use the samples to get started hooking things up:

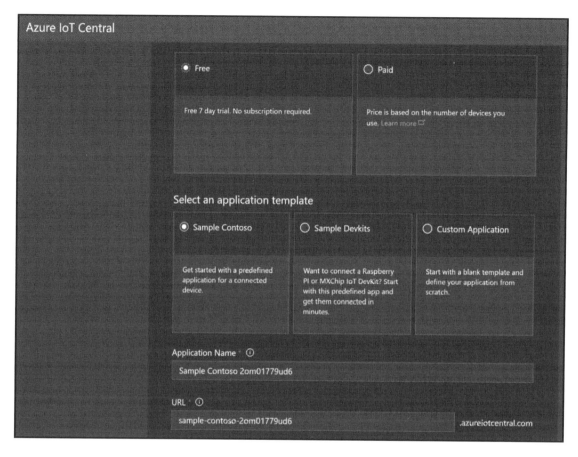

Add your device, then work on an application POC. You will work off the following dashboard:

This is a great way to not only learn but also to leverage IoT in Azure. Let's look at how an architecture might look for an IoT device:

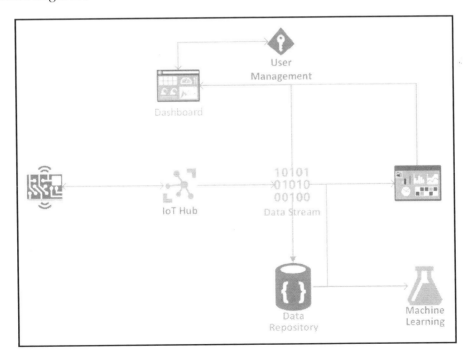

You can connect as many IoT devices as needed to this model and you can leverage machine learning to tell you things about your environment and devices, such as monitoring devices for errors and predicting when failures will occur or doors left open

AI and Machine Learning

Artificial intelligence (AI), is a set of tools that allow you to make predictive models that learn. Generally, AI application leverage three key factors:

- Ingesting data from multiple connected sources
- Building a model and training the data
- Deploying the model and tracking

The AI services in the cloud come in a few versions. Let's take a quick look:

- **Pre-built**: These are as-a-service offerings. The types are as follows:
- **Vision**: Used to identify and analyze image content.
- **Speech**: To convert the spoken word to text.
- **Language**: To understand the meaning behind a speaker's intent.
- **Knowledge**: Knowledge-based services.
- **Search**: Search-based services.
- **Custom**: It allows you to rapidly prototype your own model. Great information is available at `https://docs.microsoft.com/en-us/azure/machine-learning/service/`.
- Azure Machine Learning.
- Visual Studio Code Tools for AI.
- Machine Learning Studio.
- Conversational; the bot side of the world to naturally interact with folks.
- **Bot Service**: Interactive bot that can answer questions.
- Language Understanding
- **QnA Maker**: A question and answer maker

AI has a lot of real-world uses, such as predictive maintenance and defect detection. Bots also provide tons of interaction scenarios and you can use cognitive services with your apps, including SaaS solutions. I have used the speech service in D365 for dictation for a healthcare app and I have used search to rapidly search data repositories. It has also been used to enhance how developers write code.

So, when you want to build or leverage a cognitive service, let's look at the dashboard:

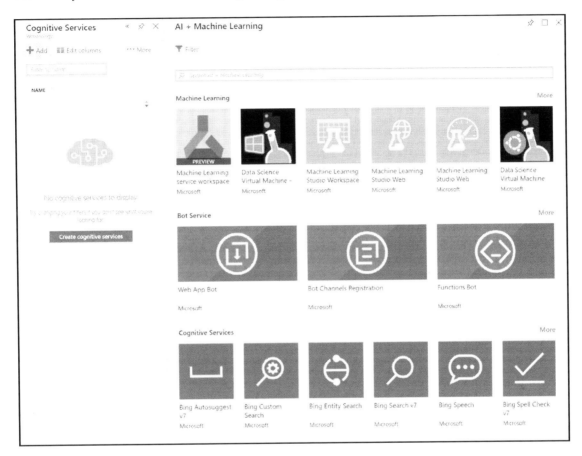

You can see that there are a lot of services and ways to interact and leverage AI. Later in this book, we will discuss how to use these services when developing solutions.

Understanding responsibility

Before we dive in, let's discuss how responsibilities are assigned in Azure and what it means to choose IaaS, PaaS, or SaaS solutions. In the following figure, there is a simplified view of Microsoft's responsibilities:

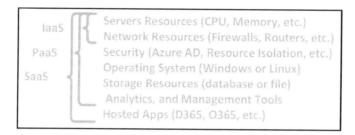

Microsoft responsibilities simplified

Let's look at some pros and cons based on responsibilities.

Infrastructure as a Service

IaaS is the simplest way to move or create an environment in Azure because this provides more synergy with the on-premise model. It can be the most costly as well for supporting resources, but the most versatile. Let's look at some pros and cons of using IaaS:

- **Pros**
  - More control over the environment
  - Simple migration to the cloud, better compatibility with legacy code
- **Cons**
  - Need to continue to patch OS
  - Need to support network configuration
  - Need more support in the environment

Platform as a Service

PaaS provides some great overall services but will limit you in language and resources used. This provides a consumption model that help drives down overall cost. Let's look at some pros and cons of using PaaS:

- **Pros**
    - Automatic updates
    - Cost reduction, only pay for what you use
    - Assured compatibility, closed ecosystem
- **Cons**
    - Locked into a specific development practice

Software as a Service

SaaS, involves pre-made software solutions that can provide a distinctly quicker time to market. Software packages include Dynamics 365, Office 365, and SharePoint to name a few. Let's look at some pros and cons of using SaaS:

- **Pros**
    - Can be accessed from anywhere
    - Reduced cost, mostly per seat licensing
    - Better reliability
    - Simplified management
    - Speed to market
    - Scalability
- **Cons**
    - Downtime and outages
    - Security, vendor-specific in cases
    - Locked into a vendor
    - Reduced control
    - Compliance
    - Performance

Azure Active Directory

Azure Active Directory, also referred to as Azure AD/AAD, is Microsoft's multi-tenant identity management for all it's tenant resources and services. It provides Single Sign-On, or SSO, services for operations folks and Application Identity services for the developers. It comes in the following four flavors and provides three 9s or 99.9% SLA and pricing (https://azure.microsoft.com/en-us/pricing/details/active-directory/):

- Free
- Basic - $1 per user:
    - Cost-reducing features such as group-based access management
    - Self-service password reset for cloud applications
    - Azure Active Directory Application Proxy
- P1 - $6 per user:
    - All basic features
    - Hybrid environments across application access
    - Self-service identity
    - Access management (IAM)
    - Identity protection
- P2 - $9 per user:
    - All P1 features
    - Identity protection
    - Privileged identity management

Other Active Directory Services that are provided through **pay as you go** are **Business to Customer (B2C)** (https://docs.microsoft.com/en-us/azure/active-directory-b2c/), and **multi-factor authentication** (https://docs.microsoft.com/en-us/azure/active-directory/authentication/concept-mfa-howitworks). As we begin this journey, I would recommend you first start by creating a plan of governance to help guide your overall Azure adoption. Let's look at how we approach this in Azure.

Plan for success

A journey without a plan is a walkabout. I once shared a story about taking a group out into the center of an open field and said—*on your marks, get set, go*. At that point everyone started running in every direction, then one turned around an said—*where is the finish line?* You see I had a vision I did not share and the participants couldn't plan, not only where they were running, but how to dress for it. So, as you can see things can get crazy when you don't plan and set the proper expectations. This is the same thing when you move to Azure; you want to ensure success with a plan/governance.

Most organizations I have seen don't spend the time creating the governance and end up having systems and applications that leave them open to vulnerabilities that are not managed properly. **Scaffolding** is used in Azure to create a structure that allows admins to ensure workloads meets minimum requirements in accordance with the plan/governance. This will hopefully create minimum interference with meeting goals quickly. I have already discussed the importance of subscriptions, resource groups, and naming conventions but let's look at some other important things to note.

To extend the conversation on resources, I recommend creating policies to help control the resource that engineers are able to deploy. You can also combine auditing features to help create a well-rounded view. This can help with Geo-compliance and data sovereignty by restricting the region's resources can be deployed. This can also help with cost management by restricting the types of resources that can be deployed. This can also extend to resource tags, which can help with auditing.

Resource tags are a way to group resources together by feature or department, for example. You can leverage then to create chargeback views to departments. To help with a naming convention, review the documentation at https://docs.microsoft.com/en-us/azure/architecture/best-practices/naming-conventions.

Create a Resource Policy that mandates tags for your Azure resources, which can be used across subscriptions.

One of the biggest things I have leverage in Azure to protect deletion of my resources, which I believe most don't know about, is Azure resource locks, which can be applied to subscriptions, resource groups, and resources. I use them in production environments to keep people from deleting resources accidentally. Resource locks currently have two values—CanNotDelete and ReadOnly. CanNotDelete means that a resource can be read and modified but not deleted. ReadOnly means a resource can be modified or deleted. As we move forward, we need to understand architectural styles, so let's dive into that.

Let's talk architecture styles

As the cloud movement takes shape, gone are the days of monolithic enterprise applications, and in step smaller decentralized services. Applications have become more asynchronous and scale both horizontally and vertically, with deployments becoming more automated and predictable. With Azure, there are certain architectural styles that are commonly leveraged, and while these styles don't rely on a specific technology, there are some technologies that fit into these architectures well.

Common application patterns

Let's take a look at a few common patterns in Azure:

- **Microservices:** Small, independent services that implement a single business function. They contain the code, configuration, and data repository needed to support the service. They are small pieces of Lego you can leverage to build applications that are team agnostic and are updated often with little to no application impact. The following are examples of microservice resources in Azure:
    - Service Fabric
    - Functions
    - WebJobs
    - Kubernetes
    - Container Services
    - Container Instances
- **Tiered:** These are the applications that are broken up into layers, such as presentation, business logic, and data access. They require a bit of coordination to update, and each layer can have an impact on other development teams. The following are examples of tiered resources for Azure:
    - App Services
    - VMs

- **Messaging:** These are pub/sub or Web-Queue-Worker models that use queues to process message tasks. These can be long-running and involve workflows in their processing structures. I lump these together because they are asynchronous message processes at the end of the day. The following are examples of messaging resources for Azure:
  - IoT Hub
  - Service Bus
  - Logic Apps
  - Storage Queues

One of the things I learned in approaching Azure is that it challenged my thoughts on architecture. These changes contained constraints on how I approached design. This made me think about my approaches in a different light, causing me to need to understand the underlying principles and the constraints behind the style. When looking at these design constraints, it was important to note the trade-offs and that styles may change based on the challenges you're looking to work through. I learned to apply my simplistic approach to not create complexity within my application domain so that I can manage dependencies cleanly. I also needed to decouple communication using asynchronous messaging, which helped with reliability and scalability. With Azure being a closed ecosystem, one of the biggest takeaways for me is how to manage the applications, which included monitoring, alerting, and logging. Now that we understand the basic architectural styles, we need to understand the technology behind our design.

How to make technology choices

Since we learned about our as-a-service model in Azure in `Chapter 1`, *Getting Started with Azure*, here, we will look at how to choose compute resources in the IaaS and PaaS models. Some mainstream compute options in Azure include Virtual Machines, App Services, Service Fabric, and Container Services. When you are selecting a compute option, you will want to consider cost, hosting, availability, and scaling. Some services, such as Azure Functions, have a true consumption model, such as pay for use. This carries its own issues on shared infrastructure, such as cold starts and so on. Azure functions can also be VM or App Plan backed with dedicated resources. So, in this example, hosting is shared, the cost is minimal, and availability and scale are based on shared services. The App Plan or VM backed pricing goes up with dedicated resources and more controllable scale.

Code in compute resources or services should be deployed and maintained via a DevOps practice, which we will cover in later chapters. The following diagram is a little compute cheat sheet I like to use when choosing a compute service as I begin my design:

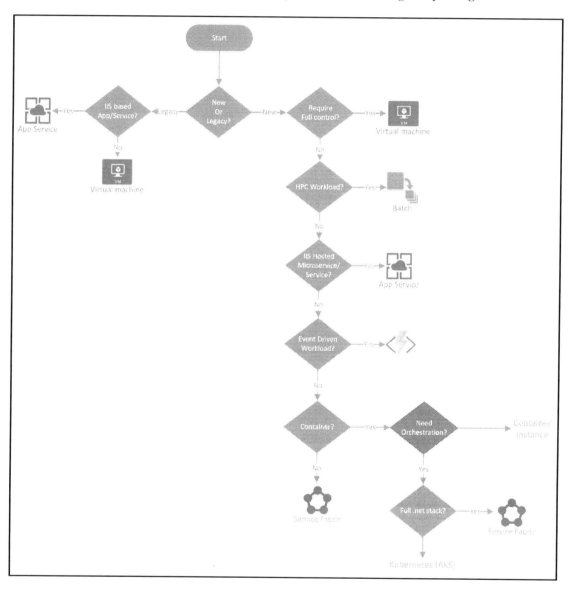

How to select a resource cheat sheet

Compute services generally require a data store, and the requirements for this data are increasing in larger and larger volumes every year. This data can trigger various business behaviors and require auditing and security at its core. With this in mind, a single data approach is not the best approach as we begin our journey. We now have a schema and schemaless data structures. But as our journey expands, as do the types of data stores available to you, you should take a moment to understand which model or combination of models best suits your application:

Relational	• Conforms to ACID (Atomic, Consistent, Isolated, Durable) • Use when strong consistency is needed • New transaction isolation • Tried and true data storage
Key/Value	• Hash table-based • Key/value paired • Value is a blob • Optimized for lookup • Highly scalable • Can be distributed across multiple nodes
Document	• Like key/value, stores named field elements (documents) • Document data can be queried • Document data doesn't need to be the same across all documents
Object	• Used to store large binary objects • Consists of a unique ID, metadata, and stored data
Files	• Same as an object but for files specifically

Now that we have discussed some technologies to use when looking at designing applications for Azure, let's look at some designs that I think are very useful.

Designing applications in Azure

I like to design applications for more scale, resilience, and manageability. Here are some things to keep in mind:

- Make your applications self-healing as much as possible:
    - Design for failures and handle them
    - Log and monitor
- Build for scaling out:
    - Offload resource intensive tasks
    - Design for scale in
    - Identify bottlenecks

- Partition around resource limits:
  - Understand limits and use partitioning to get around them; you can find more information at the following link: `https://docs.microsoft.com/en-us/azure/azure-subscription-service-limits`

- Design with DevOps in mind:
  - Monitoring
  - Deploying
  - Escalation
  - Security/auditing
  - Make all thing observable
  - Treat configuration as code
- Design for evolution:
  - Use loose coupling
  - Use asynchronous development patterns whenever possible
  - Use interfaces
  - Design for testing
  - Deploy services independently

There are a magnitude of design patterns to choose from. If you're finding it hard to decide which one to use, you can review them at `https://docs.microsoft.com/en-us/azure/architecture/patterns/`.

As we move forward, having discussed some common design approaches, Azure also enhances the five pillars of software development. Let's see what are they:

- Scalability
  - Horizontal scale: This is elastic and can be triggered automatically. It is also more cost-effective than vertically scaling.
  - Vertical scale: Can increase the resources assigned to a resource.
  - Scalability Checklist Document: `https://docs.microsoft.com/en-us/azure/architecture/checklist/scalability`.
  - Scalability Design Patterns for Performance: `https://docs.microsoft.com/en-us/azure/architecture/patterns/category/performance-scalability`.

- Availability
    - Defined by resources
    - Availability Design Patterns: `https://docs.microsoft.com/en-us/azure/architecture/patterns/category/availability`

- Resiliency
    - Closely related to Availability
    - Resiliency Design Patterns: `https://docs.microsoft.com/en-us/azure/architecture/resiliency/index`

- Management
    - Leverage DevOps in your software development
    - Use instrumentation
    - Visualize and alert
    - Analysis and diagnose
    - Monitoring Design Patterns: `https://docs.microsoft.com/en-us/azure/architecture/patterns/category/management-monitoring`

- Security
    - Identity management using Azure AD as much as possible
    - Use RBAC as much as possible to protect the infrastructure
    - Secure your applications
    - Use data encryption whenever possible
    - Security Center: `https://azure.microsoft.com/en-us/services/security-center/`
    - Security Documents: `https://docs.microsoft.com/en-us/azure/security/`
    - Microsoft Trust Center: `https://docs.microsoft.com/en-us/azure/security/`

One of the most crucial choices you have to make when building solutions on Azure is whether or not you are working with sensitive information. If the information is sensitive in nature or falls under **Personally Identifiable Information (PII)**, **Health Insurance Privacy and Portability Act (HIPPA)**, or GDFR, you will need to look at isolated networks environments in Azure. These choices come with consequences, even in closed ecosystems, as you will need to manage things like access (firewalls) and load balancing. However, you do gain extended isolation and can extend your internal network into this more secure piece of Azure.

Several environments fit into this, such as **App Service Environment** (**ASE**), Service Fabric, Custom VNets, and so on. It is crucial to understand this as this can drive cost. Isolated environments cost a significant amount more, not only from an Azure perspective but from an organization perspective (as there are more components in Azure to manage).

As fast as Azure changes, I typically look for opportunities to leverage the best of breed to solve issues. Typically, you will look up things based on what you are used to using internally, and Azure offers a bit more. So, when I typically want to do something in Azure, I look for what I am looking to accomplish, not what I am looking to do. For example, I may not look up how to store large amounts of data in SQL and look more at how to store telemetry data in Azure for IoT devices. This opened my eyes to the IoT hub as a transport and CosmosDB, which had the added benefit of speed.

Some of my thoughts on selecting resources in Azure

Basically, there is not really a silver bullet as to how to solve problems using Azure, and I believe you should approach things in a way that makes sense for you. I wanted to run through a few of the resources that I leverage a lot in Azure. With that being said, here is how I work at approaching things. Most of the time, the direction I choose in Azure is based on the organization/team I am working with and their overall core competency. This means that if I am working with a .NET or JavaScript shop, I will pick solutions that align with these, like using Node.js over C# for the JavaScript shop. I sometimes look at the need to leverage multiple cloud models, like deploying to Azure and AWS.

First and foremost, I always start with DevOps in mind, which leads to developing solutions with deploy-ability and support-ability in mind. I would at least leverage Application Insights for logging and configure it for all my resources by default. Application Insights is like the Event Log in Azure. If you don't take these to heart, supporting your applications in Azure can be very difficult to diagnose.

 Use Application Insights for all your resources to make your life easier when supporting your application. For more information, go to `https://docs.microsoft.com/en-us/azure/application-insights/app-insights-overview`.

App Services

For web solutions, I generally use App Services or Container Instances, depending on whether I am deploying as a .NET package or a Docker container. As a quick side note, App Service now encapsulates Container, Logic, and Function App services. The use of Docker containers allows for the deployment model to not be cloud-specific or require application updating because all the code and its dependencies are usually self-contained within the Docker container. When I need to create a web service (web API) or better yet, an endpoint, I would traditionally choose to redeploy it to an App Service or convert it to a function or a Logic App. A function is an App Service that can be run serverless or VM backed, and are basically small microservices. Functions were designed to run stateless, quick, small pieces of code that are trigger by an event like a timer or endpoint call execution. When the need arises to run long-running transactions, you can leverage either Web-Jobs or Logic Apps, which were designed for this purpose. So, as you can see, App Services can leverage a variety of languages and offer multiple ways to solve issues. You can also leverage isolated App Services for App Services that use PII or GDFR.

When building or hosting web applications within App Services, the infrastructure supports both Windows and Linux with auto-scaling and high availability; let's look at how the resources pan out. App Services are controlled by App Service Plans, these plans can be shared with multiple App Services; however, I recommend in most scenarios you to do one App Service per App Service Plan to maintain better application isolation for scaling. The reason for this is that the App Service is the scalable part of App Service, so any applications can use the App Service Plan scale with the App Service Plan, which may or may not be intended. Each App Service defines the following:

- Instances of application code
- Instance size
- Region hosted in
- Resource pricing tier and features

Now, instance scale is based on the pricing tier you choose, so let's look at the pricing tiers first, which will be focused on Windows-based App Services as the Linux model is still maturing in Azure and only has free for 30 days on the lowest B1 tier at the moment:

- Shared compute resources fall within the Free (F1) or the Shared (D1) tiers under the Dev/Test workload tab, as we can see in the following figure. These resources are shared and don't scale, so with this fact I would only use them for Dev/QA App Services. If you need to leverage a custom domain, I would use D1; however, you can leverage an SSL Cert, so if that is a requirement I stay in the F1 tier and the underlying Azure Website cert, or move out of the Shared Compute tier. As you can see, for the ability to add a custom domain, there is a price increase:

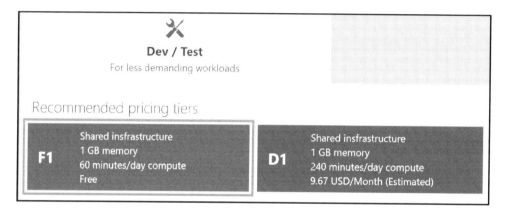

Shared compute pricing tier

Shared compute hosting plans are run on a shared VM with other customers and are not intended to run production workloads.

- Dedicated compute resources include Basic (B1-3), Standard (S1-3), Premium (P1-3), and Premium V2 (P1V2 – 3V3). These resources run on Azure VMs, which we refer to as VM backed. App Plans can share their resources with other App Services, which is different from the F1 and D1 tiers. Dedicated compute introduces the ability to use custom SSL (B1 or above), instances (scale out), deployment slots, traffic manager, and daily backups. Let's look at the Production Workload tab in the following figure:

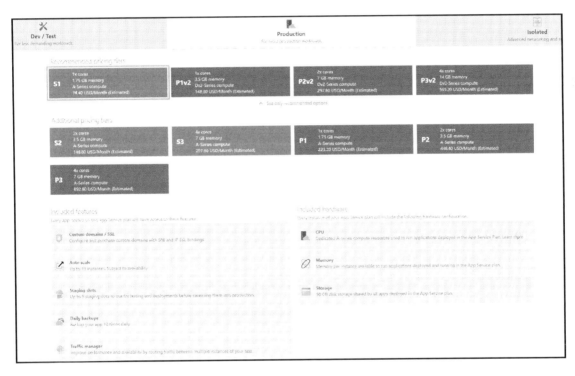

Production Workload tab

- Isolated compute is provided by Isolated (I1-3) tiers that exist within ASE, which are privately dedicated resources that are used to isolate sensitive data applications such as PII OR GDFR. Single-tenant system, Isolated network, Private app access, and max scale (up to 100 instances) are introduced in this pricing tier. Let's look at the pricing tier in the following figure for isolated resources:

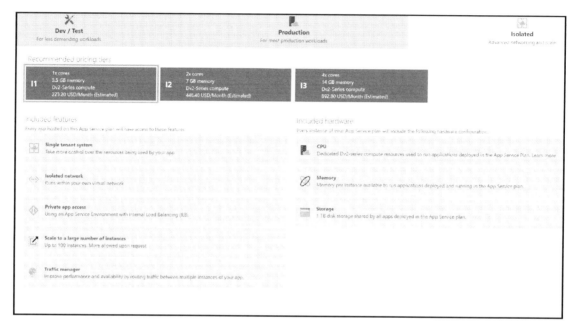

Isolated workload tier

- The Consumption tier was introduced in App Services when they moved Function Apps under App Services. The scaling is dynamic depending on the workload and is truly utility based, that is, you pay for what you use. It does, however, suffer from cold starting.

The dedicated tiers are in three sizes:

- **Small**: 1x core with 3.5 GB memory
- **Medium**: 2x cores with 7 GB memory
- **Larger**: 4x cores with 14 GB memory

Remember, as you scale out the pricing is per instance increases so the pricing tier x time number of instances will be your monthly cost as you can see in the following screenshot, which is good to understand before turning on Auto-Scale. The charges are compiled hourly and the isolated compute includes a worker in addition to a base hourly fee for the isolated resources:

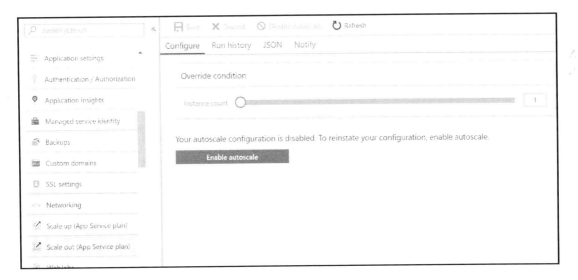

App Service scaling

The features included, such as App Service Domains and App Service Certs, are at an additional cost. App Service Certs are issued by GoDaddy and are rotated for you each year without the need for you to remember to order the cert.

Using App Service Certs, while rotated for you, still requires a refresh with the App Service to get the new version in the Key Vault.

As you can see, App Services have a variety of option to choose from, including the types of App Services you can choose from, such as WebJobs, functions, Logic Apps, Containers, and so on.

Database services

For database solutions, I generally look at SQL/MySQL (transactional) or CosmosDB (schemaless). I use CosmosDB mostly for telemetry data from devices and SQL/MySQL for transactional data that usually originates from web forms or file loads. When I need to load data, I will usually use Azure Batch or HPC (Hi Performance Compute). With SQL managed instances, I can move an existing database to the cloud for legacy databases or I can migrate more modern databases to the cloud. For more on migration planning, go to `https://docs.microsoft.com/en-us/azure/dms/tutorial-sql-server-to-azure-sql`.

When you work with SQL in Azure, you will create a main central administration point or server, which is a container for single or elastic databases. This container controls the firewall rules, auditing rules, threat detection policies, and failover groups. Data is stored with **Transparent Data Encryption** (**TDE**), by default, which encrypts your data at rest.

These are the data repository types:

- **Single database**: Own set of resources managed via an administration server
- **Elastic database**: With a shared set of resources managed via an administration server
- **Manage instances**: Contains system and user databases and shares a set of resources

Pricing for single or elastic SQL databases is based on **Data Transfer Units** (**DTUs**), and they represent the resource power assigned to the database. They are a blended measurement of memory, CPU, and read-write. Elastic instances use an elastic version, which provides a range of shared resources that cannot be consumed by a single database but ensure that the pool always has a minimum available.

The Azure DTU calculator is a great tool for calculating the DTU needed and can be found at `http://dtucalculator.azurewebsites.net/`. Also, remember Single database have limits by tier: **Basic** (2 GB size, 5 DTUs), **Standard** (1 TB size, 3000 DTUs), and **Premium** (4 TB size, 4000 DTUs). For eDTUs, the limits are **Basic** (2 GB size, 156 GB pool size, 5 eDTU/DB, 1600 eDTUs/pool, 500 DB/pool), **Standard** (1 TB size, 4 TB pool size, 3000 eDTU/DB, 3000 eDTUs/pool, 500 DB/pool), and **Premium** (1 TB size, 4 TB pool size, 4000 eDTU/DB, 4000 eDTUs/pool, 100 DB/pool).

Managed SQL instances are based on vCores, were created for the lift and shift database model, and were put in place to "as is" data migration to Azure with no database or application updating needed, except for configuration changes. This model is based on VM instance resources, cores, and memory, to support the pricing tiers shown in the following figure:

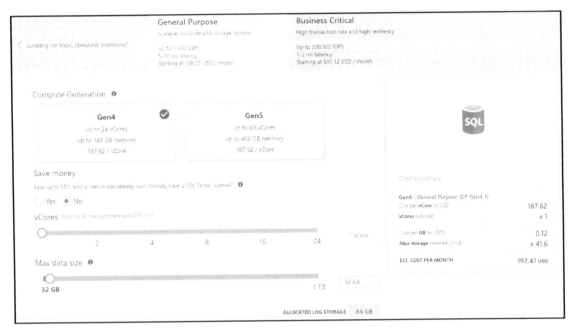

Manage Instance pricing

There are two service tiers:

- **General Purpose**: Typical availability and common IO latency requirements
- **Business Critical**: High availability and low IO latency requirements

Storage accounts

Storage accounts were put into place to help provide a filesystem style structure for data/blob object repositories in the cloud. Their pricing tiers cover physical storage and ingress/egress. These data objects are usually stored in the following fashion:

- Azure blobs are used for text and binary data
- Azure files are for file shares in the cloud
- Azure Queues are used for reliable messaging
- Azure tables are for the schema-less storage of structured data

There are currently two types storage media:

- **Standard**: Storage on magnetic storage devices
- **Premium**: Storage on SSD

All data is written to the stores with **Storage Service Encryption** (**SSE**) and can leverage RBAC from AAD to manage access.

 You will need to manage CORS rules for your resource that access resources from other domains. CORS, or Cross-Origin Resource Sharing, is not an authentication mechanism but an access one from other domains.

They have three storage account options:

1. General Purpose v2 (GPv2): Support all the latest features, and you can choose better hot and cold storage tiers
2. General Purpose v2 (GPv1): For high churn or read rates
3. Blob Storage: Supports all blob features

Let's take a look at pricing for storage and data transfers into Azure.

- Azure Storage Pricing: https://azure.microsoft.com/en-us/pricing/details/storage/
- Data Transfer Pricing: https://azure.microsoft.com/en-us/pricing/details/bandwidth/

CosmosDB

The pricing of this flexible globally distributed multi-model data store is based on **Request Units (RU/s)**. This is a throughput charge for read, write, and query operations and has a minimum of 400 RUs. There is a secondary charge for SSD storage of data. With CosmosDB being a premium service in Azure, it can get more costly. You can also replicate globally, as you can see in the following figure:

CosmosDB global view

 I have learned that missteps in using CosmosDB can be costly. One main thing I had to learn to help with this is to read the x-ms-retry-after-ms header when my RU quota was exceeded.

Like SQL, CosmosDB data collections scale by the collection/repository, as you can see in the following figure. You can adjust your RUs assigned to your collection from this view. It's good to keep an eye on the daily spend to get an estimate of monthly burn:

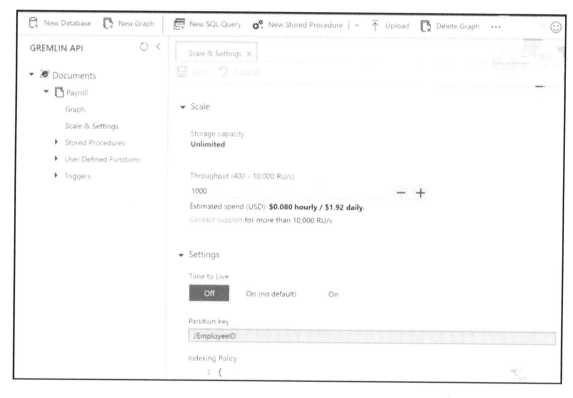

CosmosDB RUs

CosmosDB leverages Azure Functions for a trigger on database inserts or updates. Azure functions are small serverless pieces of code.

Microservices/containers

Most of the microservices in Azure will leverage App Services; however, you may need a better management service, such as Kubernetes or Service Fabric. **Service Fabric** is basically Microsoft's version of a microservice and container manager that helps with the management of multiple microservices. Service Fabric can automatically heal and manage you microservices in a single location. Kubernetes runs the same as Service Fabric but is mainly for container support. Both of these environments are expensive to run as they require the VM scale set, a load balancer, and routing under the hood to run.

Real-world examples

I had an organization that wanted to move their web applications to Azure but left their database and internal services within their infrastructure. Let's see how I solved this in the following screenshot:

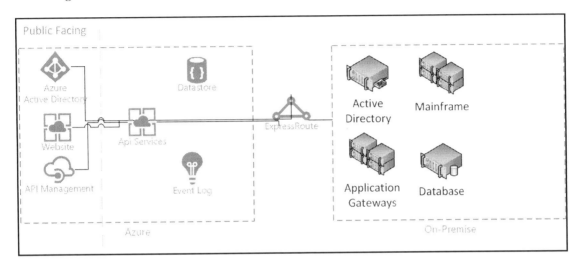

Real-world example

We moved all the websites and middle tier web services to Azure. We then re-exposed the web services using API management so that we could consume them in different formats. Azure API management is resources in Azure that allow you to proxy incoming calls of different formats to a specific format that the endpoint is expecting without rewriting the code. It is like having an XML endpoint and using API Management to accept JSON that would be transformed to XML and passed to the endpoint as XML. Express Route was used to securely connect the internal network to an Azure VNet. We then used Application Insights to store all events and exceptions.

Summary

As you can see, designing applications for Azure has it's own challenges, and there are quite a few that need mastering. Some of the biggest things to get used to are the closed ecosystem and that you will need to trust that some things are handled by Azure and are abstracted from your view. It is also important to note that applications can use multiple patterns to achieve their end goals.

In the next chapter, we will take a look at how we begin tapping into all this power within Azure.

Questions

Let's take a look at what we have learned in this chapter:

1. What does Dev/Test pricing offer?
2. Can you name something in Azure that doesn't span subscriptions?
3. What are some common architectural styles in Azure?
4. What is an ASE?

Further reading

Azure documentation: https://docs.microsoft.com/en-us/azure/

4
Understanding the Infrastructure behind Solutions Built in Azure

In prior chapters, we have touched on the ARM template process, but we will look a little further into it in this chapter. There are things you should understand in developing an application in Azure—learning how to leverage ARM templates and infrastructure as code. Help with adopting standards to provide guidance on resource usage in Azure.

The following are the topics covered in this chapter:

- Guidance for building solutions in Azure
- Understand infrastructure as code
- Configuring workloads in Visual Studio
- Testing solutions locally and in Azure

Technical requirements

The following are the requirements for this chapter:

- **Azure Architecture Guide:** `https://docs.microsoft.com/en-us/azure/architecture/guide/`
- **Free Offers:** `https://visualstudio.microsoft.com/free-developer-offers/`
- **Azure DevOps:** `https://dev.azure.com/`
- **ARM Template:** `https://docs.microsoft.com/en-us/azure/azure-resource-manager/`
- **SDKs:** `https://docs.microsoft.com/en-us/azure/index#pivot=sdkstools`

- **Azure Pricing Calculator:** `https://azure.microsoft.com/en-us/pricing/calculator/`
- **Azure Subscriptions:** `https://account.windowsazure.com/Subscriptions`

Setting up your development environment

As we begin developing solutions, you can install Visual Studio or Visual Studio Code as well as create an Azure DevOps account. You can find the downloads at `https://visualstudio.microsoft.com/free-developer-offers/` and for the purposes of this book, we are going to stick with Visual Studio over Visual Studio Code. In Visual Studio, please ensure the following Workloads are installed:

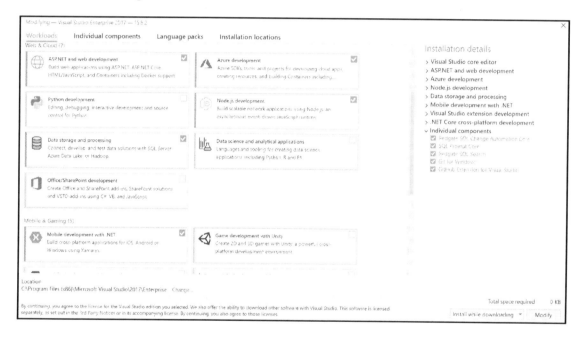

Visual Studio Workloads for Azure Development

Now that you have installed/verified Visual Studio, let's head over to Azure DevOps at `https://dev.azure.com/`, and sign in with the Microsoft or organization account you would like to associate with Azure DevOps. Let's walk through setting it up.

1. Click on **Continue** to accept the terms and the Code of Conduct, as you can see in the following figure:

Azure DevOps Agreement

2. You can then create a **Public** or **Private** project, as you can see in the following figure. **Public** is for anyone to access and **Private** is for folks you assign. In most situations, you will use **Private** unless you are creating a community development project:

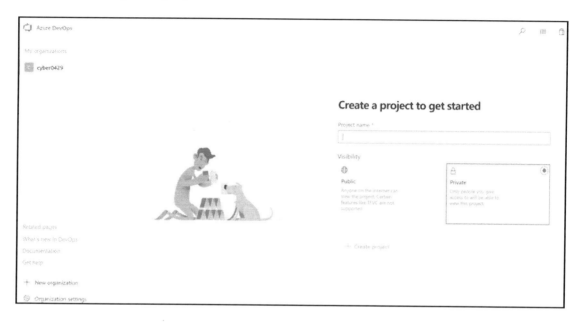

Create a project

Now, you are ready to develop solutions leveraging Azure. As we begin, we will focus on web and mobile development to keep the code samples simple for this book. While doing this, we will leverage a service-oriented approach. Now, as we discussed in prior chapters, you can choose your options to deploy, based on your comfort level, as you can see in the following figure:

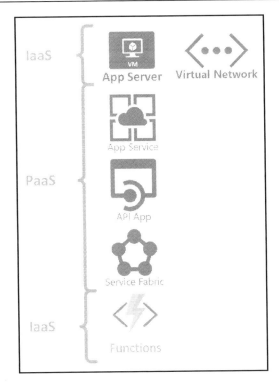

Choices for App Deploys

Your data repository can be your traditional SQL or you can opt for a NoSQL solution. I would, however, caution you against using NoSQL solutions unless you are familiar with them. They require some retry coding to reduce cost. You can also provide cloud to cloud or on-premises solution by adding Docker support, but here also I would caution you as it requires more infrastructure and a deeper understanding. So, we will stick with the tradition web application approach for simplicity and I will try to add some Docker color where I can. To review advanced SDKs, you can find more information at `https://docs.microsoft.com/en-us/azure/index#pivot=sdkstools`.

Managing cost

One of the biggest things you will need to learn is how to use the Azure pricing calculator found at `https://azure.microsoft.com/en-us/pricing/calculator/`, which you can see in the following figure:

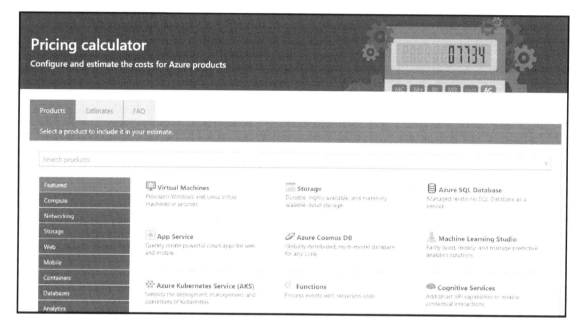

Azure Pricing Calculator

This should help you estimate your monthly burn (consumption) and it is always better to start low then scale up as needed. You can put spending limits on the account and also leverage resource tags to track spending. You can add a tag to a resource, as you can see in the following figure:

Add a Tag to an Azure Resource

But, learning will take time and we all make mistakes our first time around; I just hope you can learn from my mistakes. I would leverage free services are you learn Azure as much are you can. I would also create an alert for your burn; let's look at how.

Log into your subscriptions at `https://account.windowsazure.com/Subscriptions` and at the time of writing this book, alerts were in preview, as you can see in the following figure:

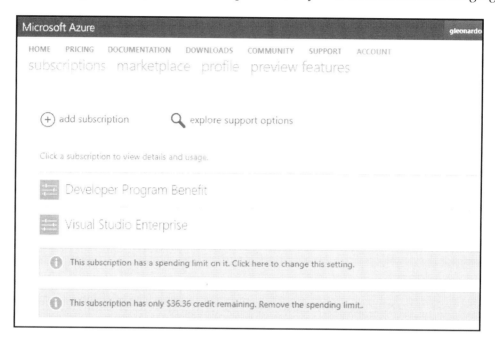

Subscription Alerts Enabled

Then you need to enable **Billing Alert Service**; once you have *enabled it* you will then see an Alerts in your subscription portal that you will configure your alert, as you can see in the following figure:

Enable Billing Alerts

Now, let's add an alert, following these steps, after the **Alerts** link is active, as in the following figure:

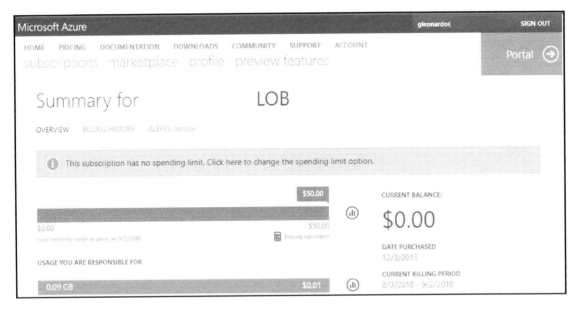

Alert link

1. Click **add alert**:

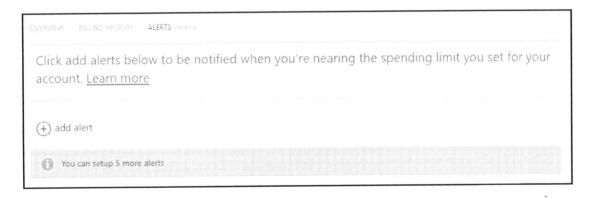

2. Add a name and set thresholds, then click **Save**:

Bingo, you now have an alert for your spending on Azure resources for that subscription. Now, let's discuss how I approach guidance for developing solutions in Azure.

How I approach guidance

When I started out in my development career, we deployed to things we controlled, such as servers or VMs within the organization. One of the biggest things I had to learn as we moved away from on-premises infrastructure, and away from VMs as a whole into the cloud, was that I don't have all the tools or logs to diagnose issues when they arise. This becomes important because while logging was important, it was often skipped because of time constraints on development. In Azure, the tools and logs are a bit harder to understand and control. You should also develop your applications to be more self-healing and fail gracefully, and if you don't plan on logging you can create issues with troubleshooting or support your applications. I personally use NLog and Application Insights to help solve these issues in Azure. They help me with monitoring and alerting, and I can also leverage Azure Monitor or OMS to bring everything together. I would at approaching the development process as you can see in the following figure:

Development process

With this software application that run-in the cloud is by nature complex software that relies on a significant amount of resources and code. So, as you develop your applications you should ensure your developers are using a production-like environment. You also want to track your technical debt. As you head down this path, you want to ensure you automate your testing and test for failures. You should also automate performance testing to identify issues early, and also with capacity testing. I love to use CI/CD processes with small incremental changes, which we will discuss in depth in future chapters.

Now, another hurdle that I had to learn is about building my infrastructure as code. In prior chapters, we had a small section on deploying a VM and a VM running SQL, but let's dive into this a little further, as we will be leveraging ARM templates as we continue our journey.

Understanding Infrastructure as Code

Before we get into ARM templates and how to use them, let's look at how you can *cheat* in creating your templates from the Azure portal when you create resources via the portal for POCs. In the blade menu, you will see an item called **Automation Scripts**. Once you click on it, you will see the following blade:

As you can see, it will give you a base for understanding, what resources went behind creating the Azure resources.

Developing locally

For those of you who don't know, each resource built in Visual Studio is able to be debugged. Some will require external installs for debugging to work fully. Let's review debugging in Visual Studio for those who are unfamiliar with it. Once you open Visual Studio and create a project, you will see a debug button and a debug file menu. One caveat is that you should make sure that you have the right startup project selected, as shown in the following screenshot:

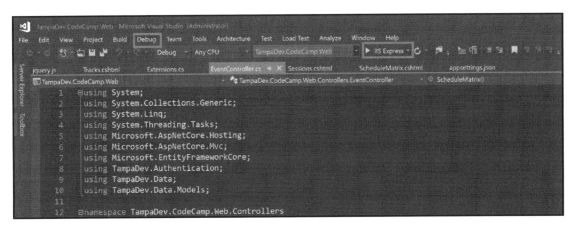

This will give you the ability to set your code with breakpoints and see what is happening. For most web applications, you can test locally, as you normally would before you deploy. I generally tend to use Docker containers to run things locally, such as testing or adding a .NET Core App to Docker. There are also some emulators to help with local development. Let's start by installing Docker locally; I would make sure that you are running Hyper-V locally or Docker will install VirtualBox as the management resource. Before you install, review the documentation at `https://docs.docker.com/docker-for-windows/install/`.. I use Docker to install things such as MongoDB, CosmosDB, and so on.

The other things I install (optional) are the following:

- **CosmosDB:** `https://docs.microsoft.com/en-us/azure/cosmos-db/local-emulator`
- **Azure Functions Runtime:** `https://docs.microsoft.com/en-us/azure/azure-functions/functions-runtime-overview`
- **Azure Logic Apps:** `https://marketplace.visualstudio.com/items?itemName=VinaySinghMSFT.AzureLogicAppsToolsforVisualStudio-18551`

This is my shortlist of extras, and as we begin to go through development, I will point out other things that I like to use to make things easier. You can install extensions through the Extension and Updates Manager that can be helpful for development, but this down to personal choice. The following screenshot shows how you would add extensions to help with development:

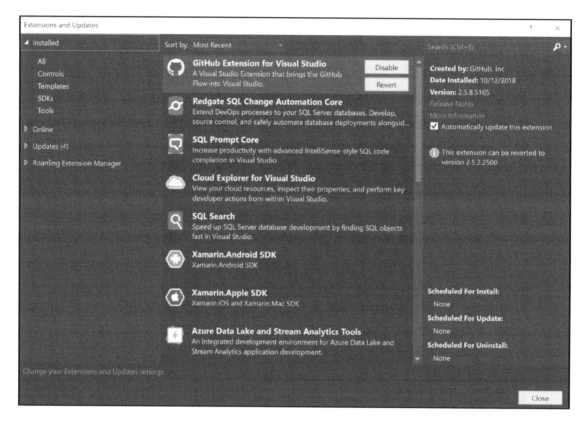

There are a lot of great extensions to use that are based on your project type. It's always good to experiment with what works for you. You can also, if you have a development subscription, deploy POCs to Azure. I like to call this my Azure Dev environment. It can help me work out issues that I may not see locally. You can do this by right-clicking on the resource you wish to publish and selecting the following instruction from the publish screen, as you can see in the following screenshot:

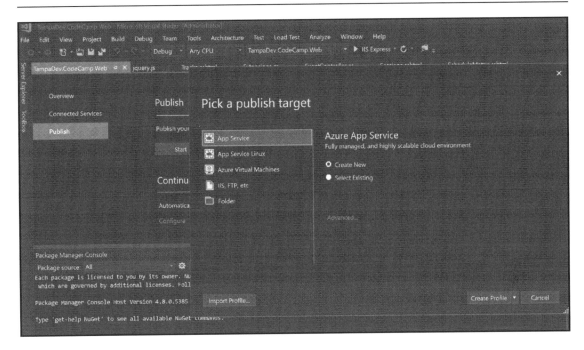

So, as you can see, your development experience can be leveraged greatly and can help you to deliver the solutions you need in Azure.

Infrastructure as Code

Now let's review what we have learned. An ARM template has a simple structure like the following:

```
{
  "$schema":
"http://schema.management.azure.com/schemas/2015-01-01/deploymentTemplate.j
son#",
  "contentVersion": "",
  "parameters": {  },
  "variables": {  },
  "functions": {  },
  "resources": [  ],
  "outputs": {  }
}
```

Expressions are written in JSON strings with brackets to start and end, and these expressions are evaluated when deployed. These are basically like JavaScript functions and are formatted like `functionname (arg1,arg2,etc)`; let's look at an example. You can develop a deeper understanding at `https://docs.microsoft.com/en-us/azure/azure-resource-manager/resource-manager-templates-variables`:

```
"variables": {
    "appServiceName": "[concat(toLower(parameters('appServiceNamePrefix')),
uniqueString(resourceGroup().id))]"
}
```

What we are doing here is setting a variable name, `appServiceName`, which is a concatenation of a parameter name and the resource group ID to make it unique. The `parameters` are sections of the template that can be tailored for, say, environment and such that can be overwritten or can contain default values. Let's look at how this would look and tie it in to the previous variable. You can develop a deeper understanding at `https://docs.microsoft.com/en-us/azure/azure-resource-manager/resource-manager-templates-parameters`:

```
"parameters": {
  "appServiceNamePrefix": {
    "type": "string",
    "defaultValue": "BookDemoAppService"
    "metadata": {
      "description": "The name prefix of the web app that you wish to
create."
    }
  },
},
```

The template system comes with some built-in templates, but you can also create your own, although there are some caveats you need to consider. Let's go over them really quickly:

- Variables and parameters cannot be accessed
- You cannot call other user-defined functions
- You cannot have default values

Let's look at a quick name creation user function. You can dive in deeper at `https://docs.microsoft.com/en-us/azure/azure-resource-manager/resource-group-authoring-templates#functions`:

```
"functions": [
  {
    "namespace": "bookdemo",
    "members": {
```

```
    "createName": {
      "parameters": [
        {
          "name": "namePrefix",
          "type": "string"
        }
      ],
      "output": {
        "type": "string",
        "value": "[concat(toLower(parameters('namePrefix')),
  uniqueString(resourceGroup().id))]"
      }
    }
  }
],
```

Let's look at how to call this function within the template.

```
"resources": [
  {
    "name": "[bookdemo.createName(parameters('webAppName'))]",
    ...
  }
]
```

The `resources` section of the template is for the resources you are looking to deploy with the template. Now, not all Azure resources can be deployed in a template; to get a deeper understanding, please review `https://docs.microsoft.com/en-us/azure/azure-resource-manager/resource-manager-templates-resources`.

You can also set up output parameters; they can be used in the deployment process to return variables from the template deployed and can be used in other parts of the release pipeline. A **release pipeline** is the thing that needs to be released by a deployment. For a deeper look at output parameters, see `https://docs.microsoft.com/en-us/azure/azure-resource-manager/resource-manager-templates-outputs`.

Let's look at how to begin creating a template in a Visual Studio project after you install the Azure Workload. In **Visual Studio**, you select **File**, then **New Project**, as you can see in the following screenshot:

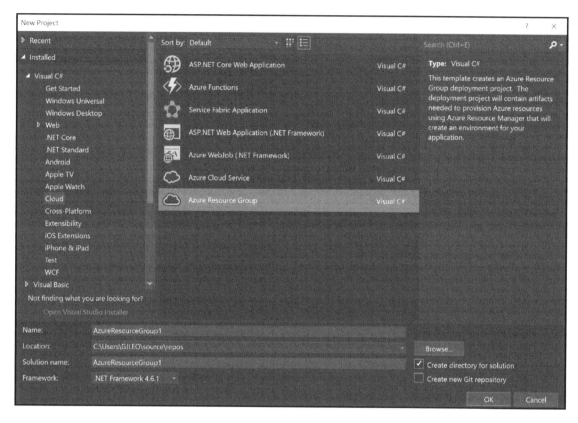

Creating an Azure Resource Group

Now that we understand how to create an ARM template, I should also mention you can link or nest templates to create a module approach to template management. You can accomplish this by adding a resource hint to the main template; let's see how we do that:

```
"resources": [
    {
        "apiVersion": "2017-05-10",
        "name": "linkedTemplate",
        "type": "Microsoft.Resources/deployments",
        "properties": {
            "mode": "Incremental",
            // Nested template or external template link //
        }
```

```
      }
   ]
```

You can add the external link to a template and parameter file as follows:

```
"templateLink": {
"uri":"https://bookdemo.blob.core.windows.net/ARMTemplates/newStorageAccoun
t.json",
          "contentVersion":"1.0.0.0"
        },
        "parametersLink": {
           "uri":"https:// bookdemo.blob.core.windows.net/ ARMTemplates
/newStorageAccount.parameters.json",
           "contentVersion":"1.0.0.0"
        }
```

 It should be noted that nested templates do not allow you to use parameters or variables that are defined within the nested template. You can, however, use them from the parent template, unless you are using an external template as defined previously.

Now, within a template, you can have a resource dependent on another resource by using the dependsOn hint, like this for a resource to be dependent on a VNet:

```
"dependsOn": [
  "[resourceId('Microsoft.Network/virtualNetworks',
variables('virtualNetworkName'))]"
  ]
```

It is added to a resource as follows:

```
{
   "type": "Microsoft.Compute/virtualMachine",
   "name": "[variables('myVMName')]",
   "location": "[variables('region')]",
   "apiVersion": "2016-03-30",
   "tags": {
     "displayName": "VMGroup"
   },
   "dependsOn": [
     "[variables('virtualNetworkName')]"
   ],
   ...
}
```

ARM templates are an important piece to learn when using Azure; you can dive deeper by reviewing the Microsoft documentation at `https://docs.microsoft.com/en-us/azure/azure-resource-manager/`.

How I develop locally

For most web applications, you can test locally, as you normally would before you deploy. I generally tend to use Docker containers to run things locally, like testing or add a .NET Core App to Docker. There are also some emulators to help with local development. Let's start by installing Docker locally; I would make sure you are running Hyper-V locally or Docker will install VirtualBox as the management resource. Before you install, review the documentation at `https://docs.docker.com/docker-for-windows/install/`. I use Docker to install things like MongoDB, CosmosDB, and so on.

The other things I install (optional) are as follows:

1. CosmosDB: `https://docs.microsoft.com/en-us/azure/cosmos-db/local-emulator`
2. Azure Functions Run-time: `https://docs.microsoft.com/en-us/azure/azure-functions/functions-runtime-overview`
3. Azure Logic Apps: `https://marketplace.visualstudio.com/items?itemName=VinaySinghMSFT.AzureLogicAppsToolsforVisualStudio-18551`

This is my short list of extras, and as we begin to go through development, I will point out other things that I like to use to make things easier.

Summary

As you can see, there are things in Azure you will want to use, such as VSTS and ARM templates. These are just new ways to do things and will take time to learn. Leveraging tools such as Docker or emulators can greatly help you deliver solutions in Azure.

Enough with the *behind the scenes* shenanigans, let's get to some development!

Questions

Let's take a look at what we have learned:

1. What are Visual Studio Workloads?
2. What does ARM stand for?
3. Which ARM template hint do you use for a dependent resource?
4. Can you nest templates?

Further reading

Azure documentation can be found here: `https://docs.microsoft.com/en-us/azure/`

5
Developing Solutions the Right Way in Azure

Now that we have a basic understanding of ARM templates and how to deploy Azure resources, let's see how to add code to them. We will understand how to develop solutions in Azure, things you have to trust, and guidance on selecting the type of resources to use in your development process. Furthermore, we will try to learn how to leverage Application Insights in your application development to help with application monitoring and support.

These topics are covered in this chapter:

- Understanding Visual Studio workloads
- Development guidance
- Leveraging Application Insights
- Selecting development resources in Azure
- On-premises to Azure integration

Technical requirements

The following are the requirements for this chapter:

- Azure Security Center: `https://docs.microsoft.com/en-us/azure/security-center/`
- Active Directory Development documentation: `https://docs.microsoft.com/en-us/azure/active-directory/develop/active-directory-appmodel-v2-overview`
- B2C Development documentation: `https://docs.microsoft.com/en-us/azure/active-directory-b2c/`

- Data Annotations: `https://docs.microsoft.com/en-us/ef/ef6/modeling/code-first/data-annotations`
- Code First for Teams: `https://docs.microsoft.com/en-us/ef/ef6/modeling/code-first/migrations/teams`
- Application Insights: `https://docs.microsoft.com/en-us/azure/application-insights/`

The developer journey

As I began my journey in software delivery, I had to learn to keep things simple, and this went against all my principles as an engineer. We engineers like to take complicated things and further complicate them. I believed the more complicated the solution, the more intelligent one looks. I came to find the error in my thought process and learned that the simplicity of things was far more important. There is an elegance to keeping development simple in software so you can provide a solution while keeping the development of that solution small in nature. This is a hard principle to convey to folks that haven't experienced the long nights and hours of pulling your hair out with complex solutions. So I now look for things with synergies to keep things simple, for instance using ASP.NET MVC and Angular; with both being MVC (Model-View-Controller) based, they play nicely together. Learning the direct connection to resources instead of keeping them decoupled gave me the ability to recover from a failure because of durable messaging queues. The moral of this babbling is the **Keep It Simple, Stupid (K.I.S.S.)** principle, which will make your life easier in Azure.

Now keep in mind that the term Workload, as we discussed in the prior chapter, is the package that is used to install resources in Visual Studio. A workload can also mean the resources in Azure that do work, such as SQL workloads or file processing workloads. It is good to learn these terms and understand how they apply to communication and understanding. It took me a while to learn that the terms you use have an effect on what people understand or take away from a conversation, and I have learned to use this terminology to keep folks on the same page.

Let's look at some choices to *lift and shift* your applications to Azure that minimize code changes. This isn't the be all and end all, but is a good starting point:

	Monolithic/ N-Tier	Mobile App Services	Microservices	Messaging Orchestration	High compute
Web Apps	X				
Mobile Apps		X			
Functions			X	X	
Logic Apps				X	
Virtual Machines	X	X		X	X
Kubernetes	X		X		
Service Fabric	X		X		
Container Instance	X		X		
Batch					X

Let's look at some lift and shift to data stores in Azure; this again isn't the be all and end all, but a good starting point:

	Relational	Unstructured	Semi-Structured	Queue	Files	High Performance	Large Data	Small Data	Geo Redundancy
SQL	X								
MySQL	X								
CosmosDB		X	X			X	X	X	X
Blob		X					X	X	X
Table			X					X	X
Queue				X				X	X
File					X		X	X	X

As a reminder, most Azure storage has **Transparent Data Encryption** (**TDE**) by default, but you want to ensure it is on.

 TDE, once turned on, encrypts data only after that point, make sure you have it turned on before you load/migrate data.

Now, as you start to work on your application, you should plan the following:

- Perform FMA (failure mode analysis):
    - Identify the types of failures
    - Plan on the effect and impact of failure
    - Identify recovery paths
- Plan on multiple instances
- Leverage auto-scaling
- Use load balancing to distribute the load
- Monitor third-party services
- Use the asynchronous development pattern as much as possible
- Leverage Dependency Injection as much as possible

Let's talk about security

While this book isn't about security, one of the main things you want to take into account when you develop solutions in the cloud is security. With that in mind, I would like to highlight some useful resources in Azure that can make your operation engineer a bit happier. You want to ensure that you create a unified approach to this, not only from a management perspective but from a threat protection perspective as well. You want to ensure that you can cover the following:

- Monitor both cloud and on-premise workloads
- Ensure standards and compliance through policies
- Find and fix vulnerabilities quickly
- Leverage access and control to limit malicious activities
- Simplify investigation with analytics and threat intelligence to detect and respond to attacks

Honorable mention – security center

To help me with this, I like using Azure Security Center. It offers a significant amount of insight into my Azure Resources and comes in two pricing tiers at the moment. I recommend the Standard tier for most organizations, as it is well worth the monthly fee, as you can see here:

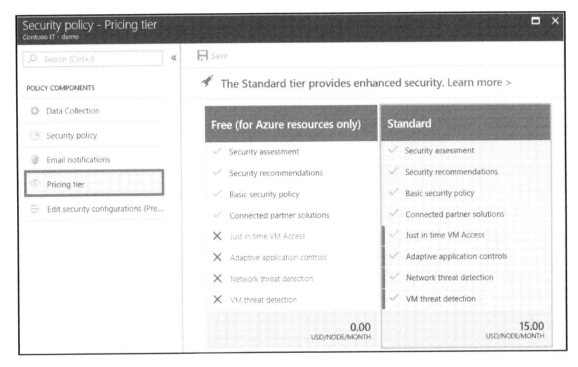

Security Center Pricing

Security Center is a useful tool, even in the free tier, to help with securing your Azure resources, or if nothing else, giving you extra eyes for security, as you can see here:

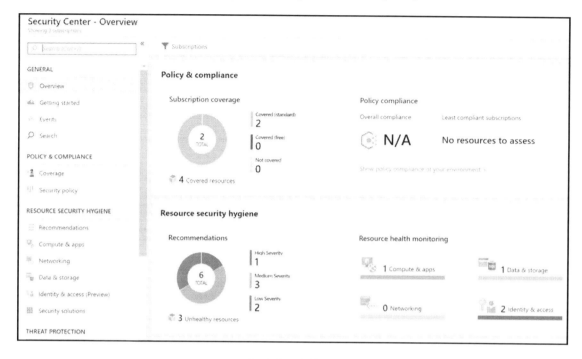

Security Center Dashboard

I would recommend you spend some time reviewing the Security Center documentation at `https://docs.microsoft.com/en-us/azure/security-center/` for a better understanding of how to use it within your organization development and operations processes. Now, let's look at application authentication. Now, for developers, there are two flavors you can choose from AAD, which is good for **internal** applications that only members of the organization need to access, and Business to Consumer, or B2C, which you can leverage for external people to access without complicating your AAD. To understand B2C it is the old Organization Unit or OU in the internal AD that isolates the members and creates an easier identity management model. Let's look at AAD first.

Application authentication

Azure Active Directory is a Microsoft identity manager and is used to create intelligence-driven access policies that are used to secure Azure resources. Every Tenant created in Azure is backed by an Azure Active Directory, which assists in the Role-Based Access Control, or RBAC, which is the identity model that Azure resource leverage for security. It is shared between both SaaS based solutions such as Office 365 and IaaS/PaaS based solutions such as App Services/VMs in Azure. Here, you can see the basic flow of a user authenticating:

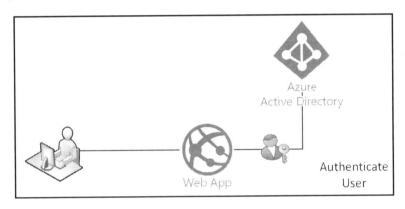

Basic Login Flow

 You need to remember all applications need to be registered with AAD. AAD supports OAuth 2.0 and OpenID Connection standards.

If you would like to dive a bit deeper into AAD and learn more about it, I would suggest you use the 2.0 endpoint documentation at `https://docs.microsoft.com/en-us/azure/active-directory/develop/active-directory-appmodel-v2-overview`. Now, let's see how we add it to your application.

First, add your **Application Registration** to AAD within the Azure portal, as you can see here:

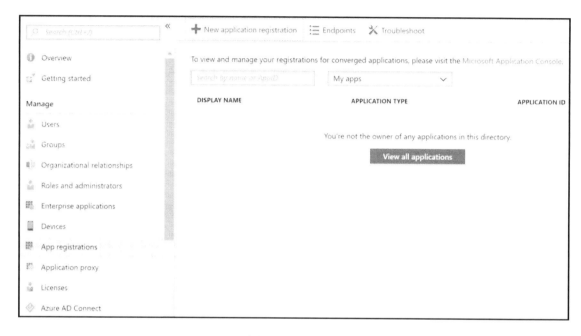

Add Application Registration

Make sure to note the **Application ID**, as you can see here. You will need this for your configuration within your application:

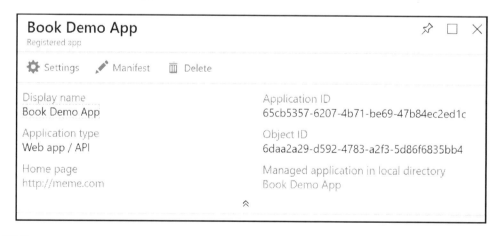

Application Registration Screen

To add security to your application, let's take a quick look at adding it to an ASP.NET MVC (Model-View-Controller) application. For the ASP.NET web application, make sure to add the following package with the package manager:

```
Install-Package Microsoft.Owin.Security.OpenIdConnect
Install-Package Microsoft.Owin.Security.Cookies
Install-Package Microsoft.Owin.Host.SystemWeb
```

 Sometimes, your application may not include a Startup.cs, so you just need to right-click on the project folder and say Add > New Item > OWIN Startup class, then name it Startup.cs.

The examples are in C# and you will need to add the following in the Startup.cs.

Update the references to include the OWIN Authentication; we will be using OpenConnectID in this example:

```
using Microsoft.Owin;
using Owin;
using Microsoft.IdentityModel.Protocols.OpenIdConnect;
using Microsoft.IdentityModel.Tokens;
using Microsoft.Owin.Security;
using Microsoft.Owin.Security.Cookies;
using Microsoft.Owin.Security.OpenIdConnect;
using Microsoft.Owin.Security.Notifications;
```

Then, in the Startup class, add these variables:

```
// This is the ApplicationID to Azure AD.
string clientId =
System.Configuration.ConfigurationManager.AppSettings["ClientId"];
// RedirectUri where the user will be redirected to after they sign in.
string redirectUri =
System.Configuration.ConfigurationManager.AppSettings["RedirectUri"];
// Your Tenant ID
static string tenant =
System.Configuration.ConfigurationManager.AppSettings["Tenant"];
// Authority is the URL for authority,
https://login.microsoftonline.com/<Tenant>/v2.0
string authority =
String.Format(System.Globalization.CultureInfo.InvariantCulture,
System.Configuration.ConfigurationManager.AppSettings["Authority"],
tenant);
```

Add this to the `Configuration` method:

```
app.SetDefaultSignInAsAuthenticationType(CookieAuthenticationDefaults.Authe
nticationType);
        app.UseCookieAuthentication(new CookieAuthenticationOptions());
        app.UseOpenIdConnectAuthentication(
            new OpenIdConnectAuthenticationOptions
            {
                ClientId = clientId,
                Authority = authority,
                RedirectUri = redirectUri,
                PostLogoutRedirectUri = redirectUri,
                Scope = OpenIdConnectScope.OpenIdProfile,
                ResponseType = OpenIdConnectResponseType.IdToken,
                TokenValidationParameters = new TokenValidationParameters()
                {
                    ValidateIssuer = false
                },
                Notifications = new
OpenIdConnectAuthenticationNotifications
                {
                    AuthenticationFailed = OnAuthenticationFailed
                }
            }
        );
```

Then, add the following method for what to do on authentication failure:

```
private Task
OnAuthenticationFailed(AuthenticationFailedNotification<OpenIdConnectMessag
e, OpenIdConnectAuthenticationOptions> context)
    {
        context.HandleResponse();
        context.Response.Redirect("/?errormessage=" +
context.Exception.Message);
        return Task.FromResult(0);
    }
```

Then, in the Home Controller, all you have to do is add the following.

Add resources for OWIN:

```
using Microsoft.Owin.Security;
using Microsoft.Owin.Security.Cookies;
using Microsoft.Owin.Security.OpenIdConnect;
```

Then, add two actions. Sign in as follows:

```
public void SignIn()
{
    if (!Request.IsAuthenticated)
    {
        HttpContext.GetOwinContext().Authentication.Challenge(
            new AuthenticationProperties{ RedirectUri = "/" },
            OpenIdConnectAuthenticationDefaults.AuthenticationType);
    }
}
```

Sign out as follows:

```
public void SignOut()
{
    HttpContext.GetOwinContext().Authentication.SignOut(
            OpenIdConnectAuthenticationDefaults.AuthenticationType,
            CookieAuthenticationDefaults.AuthenticationType);
}
```

Add the following HTML to the Home View:

```
@if (!Request.IsAuthenticated)
{
    <a href="@Url.Action("SignIn", "Home")" style="text-decoration: none;">
        <svg xmlns="http://www.w3.org/2000/svg" xml:space="preserve"
width="300px" height="50px" viewBox="0 0 3278 522" class="SignInButton">
        <style type="text/css">.fil0:hover {fill: #4B4B4B;} .fnt0 {font-
size: 260px;font-family: 'Segoe UI Semibold', 'Segoe UI'; text-decoration:
none;}</style>
        <rect class="fil0" x="2" y="2" width="3174" height="517"
fill="black" />
        <rect x="150" y="129" width="122" height="122" fill="#F35325" />
        <rect x="284" y="129" width="122" height="122" fill="#81BC06" />
        <rect x="150" y="263" width="122" height="122" fill="#05A6F0" />
        <rect x="284" y="263" width="122" height="122" fill="#FFBA08" />
        <text x="470" y="357" fill="white" class="fnt0">Sign in with
Microsoft</text>
        </svg>
    </a>
}
else
{
    <span><br/>Hello
@System.Security.Claims.ClaimsPrincipal.Current.FindFirst("name").Value;</s
pan>
    <br /><br />
```

```
    @Html.ActionLink("See Your Claims", "Index", "Claims")
    <br /><br />
    @Html.ActionLink("Sign out", "SignOut", "Home")
}
@if (!string.IsNullOrWhiteSpace(Request.QueryString["errormessage"]))
{
    <div style="background-color:red;color:white;font-weight: bold;">Error:
@Request.QueryString["errormessage"]</div>
}
```

And bingo, you now are using AAD to authenticate your user, but wait, people can still get to things without logging in. Well, now that you have created a way for people to log in, you have not yet secured your site. To do this, we want to lock it down, which can be done globally by a Controller or Action. I always recommend globally, because it is easier to loosen up security than remember to tighten it down, but let's look at how to do each way first.

To add authentication globally, add the following to `global.asa`. In the `app_start` section, add the following:

```
GlobalFilters.Filters.Add(new AuthorizeAttribute());
```

Now you will be challenging any route/action you choose from a security/logged perspective. Now, if you want to allow access to an Action, you will need to add the `[AllowAnonymous]` attribute to the Action. In this case, go to your Home Controller and the Index action, then add the `[AllowAnonymous]` attribute. You will now be able to browse to the default homepage without logging in.

This is basically how you will integrate any application into AAD. Now, B2C functions in the same way, as you will need to register the application; however, you will need to also generate a key, as you can see here:

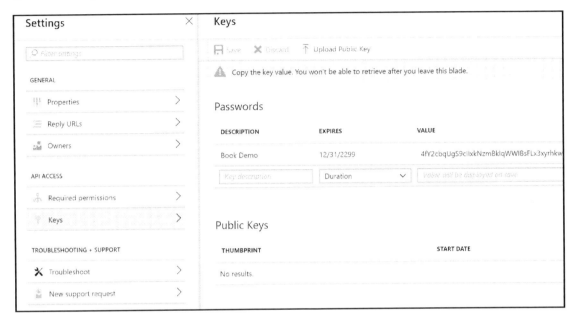

Generating a key for an Application Registration

But before we can do this, we will need to create the B2C Tenant. Remember I said that an instance of Azure Active Directory was connected to a Tenant? Well, we will need to create a new Tenant that we will use to secure our applications. To create a new B2C Tenant, click **+ Create a resource** then type **Azure Active Directory B2C** and hit *Enter*, as you can see here:

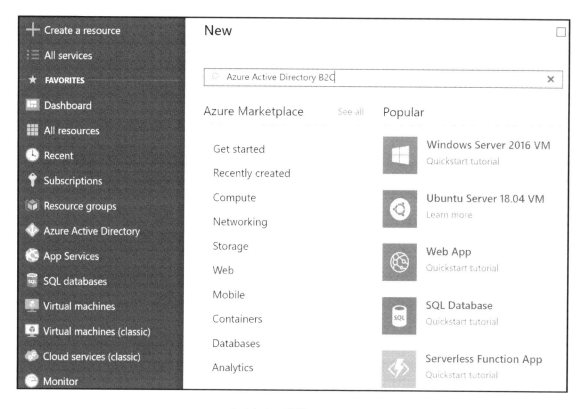

Search for Azure B2C Tenant to create

Then click **Create**, as you can see here:

Create a B2C Tenant

At this point, you can create a new B2C Tenant or link to an existing one, as you can see here. For the purposes of this discussion, we will create a new one, so click on **Create a new Azure AD B2C Tenant**:

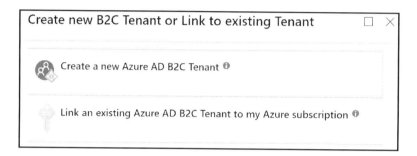

Create or Link to a B2C Tenant

Then, enter you **Organization name**, **Initial domain name**, and **Country or region**, as you can see here:

Enter new B2C Tenant information

To navigate to your new Tenant, you will need to switch over to it, as you can see here. This will function like AAD, with a few exceptions. You will need to create policies to leverage in your development, along with assigning permissions to your app service principle:

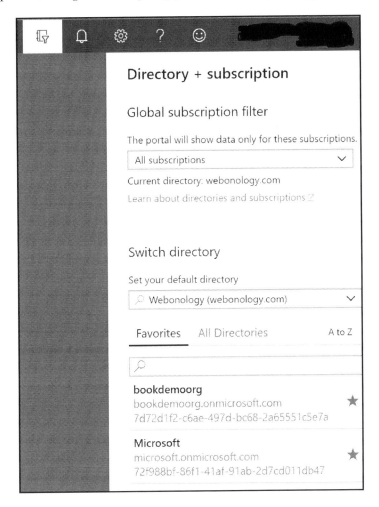

Switch to new B2C Tenant

Now, the configuration of B2C is subjective, according to the policies you want to leverage, which I wasn't looking to fully cover in this book. You can do a deeper dive into B2C at `https://docs.microsoft.com/en-us/azure/active-directory-b2c/`. I would, however, like to share some things I learned that aren't documented very well, and I would also recommend you fully research the resource you want to use in Azure to gain more knowledge about the pros and cons. We ran into an issue where the graph had issues with password changing and resetting, that drove me crazy but here is how I fixed it. Here are the PowerShell commands I ran on the B2C Tenant:

```
Connect-MsolService
$applicationId = "App ID from app you are needing to elevate permission"
$sp = Get-MsolServicePrincipal -AppPrincipalId $applicationId
# Directory Read
Add-MsolRoleMember -RoleObjectId 88d8e3e3-8f55-4a1e-953a-9b9898b8876b -
RoleMemberObjectId $sp.ObjectId -RoleMemberType servicePrincipal
# Directory Write
Add-MsolRoleMember -RoleObjectId 9360feb5-f418-4baa-8175-e2a00bac4301 -
RoleMemberObjectId $sp.ObjectId -RoleMemberType servicePrincipal
# User Account Admin - for deletes
Add-MsolRoleMember -RoleObjectId fe930be7-5e62-47db-91af-98c3a49a38b1 -
RoleMemberObjectId $sp.ObjectId -RoleMemberType servicePrincipal
```

But as you can see, security gets a bit easier in Azure and there is less to worry about once you get things set up. Now, one thing I added to my development work is **Inversion of Control (IoC)**, commonly called **Dependency Injection**.

Let's talk Dependency Injection

The purpose of **Dependency Injection (DI)**, is that the flow of control within the application is not controlled by the application but by the underlying framework. Here are some common DI frameworks and while this book isn't about telling you how to develop, I thought pointing this out will help with your overall development process:

- Castle Windsor
- Spring.NET
- Unity
- MEF
- .Net Core

I like using DI because it allows me to loosely couple code and update smaller pieces of code in the long run. It pairs itself great with the DevOps process I will discuss in the next chapter. It help with unit testing as you can use mocks to generate the implementation of the injected object.

There are three types of DI:

1. **Constructor Injection**: This requires specific values at the time of creation I order to instantiate the object. These values are provided through parameters. This is most commonly encountered when a class requires one or more dependencies. This helps by providing a strong dependency contract, and can be immutable, but also supports better testing.
   Services are resolved using two mechanisms:

   - The interface IServiceProvider
   - User-facing abstractions, such as MVC controllers or model binders, called ActivatorUtilities, which allow object creation with service registrations

2. **Setter Injection**: This allows costly resources to be created as required and as late as possible. I would like to note that dependencies can be difficult to identify, because the up-front wiring of a dependency graph is not required. You will need to NULL check before using it.

3. **Method Injection**: This is the least used DI, because it injects dependencies into a single method.

With DI, the main benefits are that your code is more testable, maintainable, reusable, and readable. So, I would recommend using DI as much as possible. One good example is injecting logging into class, which allows you to change the "where" your logs go at a whim.

Let's talk logging

Logging was one of the biggest things I had to adjust to in Azure. I was so used to being able to dig things out of a server that it was like second nature. The first time I had to dig things out of Azure due to poor logging, I went cross-eyed staring at the log stream. So, I adopted NLog because I liked how configurable it was and that it followed my DI pattern. I also learned how to use it for informational purposes, because in Azure you want to ensure your application can self-heal and/or fails gracefully, allowing developers code swallowing errors and moving on, is a bad practice. You can read the documentation on NLog at `https://nlog-project.org/` and install the NuGet package with this:

```
install-package Microsoft.ApplicationInsights.NLogTarget
```

Whether or not your use NLog, you need to make sure you are logging as much as you can to help you support your application and organization. Remember the mantra: life in Azure is always easier with logging!

Let's talk about data storage

I am one of those older developers who remember the database-first approach. I also used LINQ back in the day to load my POCO objects. Then, in stepped Entity Framework, to which I was like "hey this is awesome". Then, in steps the concept of code-first, which left me going "why?" But, I decided to give it a go and it was a great learning experience, as I found my code to be more testable as I could mock the data object, but quickly learned that updating the data model in future releases was troublesome. I then learned that migrations were one of the most important things to understand in order to be truly successful with code-first. But, one of the biggest gains was I did not need to couple to a repository and had the freedom to develop solutions with little to no concern about what my repository was. Some hard lessons that I had to learn were things like using data annotations to control my string length so my string fields wouldn't be NVARCHAR (Max). To read move on this topic, head over to `https://docs.microsoft.com/en-us/ef/ef6/modeling/code-first/data-annotations`. You can also read more on how to use code-first in a team environment at `https://docs.microsoft.com/en-us/ef/ef6/modeling/code-first/migrations/teams`.

Understanding service lifetimes

Let's take a look at the following points to better understand service lifetimes:

- Transient, great for lightweight, stateless services are created each time they are requested
- Scoped, created once per request.
- Singleton, created the first time they are requested or when ConfigureService is run. Every call subsequent call leverages the same instance.

As we discussed and looked at earlier in the chapter, selecting of your data source is a decision to be based on what you are looking to get out of it. Let's take another look below. This is how I recommend which system to use, based on functional needs:

	Relational	Unstructured	Semi-Structured	Queue	Files	High Performance	Large Data	Small Data	Geo Redundancy
SQL	X								
MySQL	X								
CosmosDB		X	X			X	X	X	X
Blob		X					X	X	X
Table			X					X	X
Queue				X				X	X
File					X		X	X	X

Azure SQL becomes your default relational data system for Azure, because it is fully managed and offers you automatic tuning and monitors. You can also leverage other systems, such as MySQL, PostgreSQL, and MariaDB as manager service,s if you are more familiar with those. In an Azure schemaless database, such as CosmosDB, have been operationalize and can be leveraged in solutions. I always challenge developers to think more deeply and understand better where they can take their development processes.

I feel it is also good to mention that, in Azure, you should make sure not to leverage traditional storage mechanisms for files, images, and so on. Often, these are things we store in file systems that may be served better in one of the Azure systems shown here:

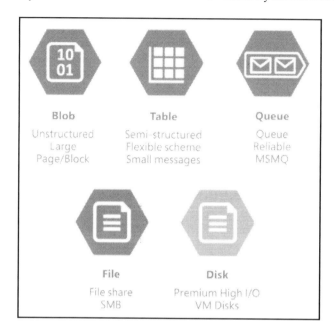

For me, I usually store images and B2C templates in Blob storage; for instance, in my Azure projects. When I need a messaging structure, I use Queues or Services Bus. If is important to understand the FTP services in Azure have been more to more secure files management system and protocol to get these files in Azure and share them.

At the end of the day, you need to pick the right repository for your needs, try not to follow the cool thing with understanding, as this is the biggest danger in Azure. I can't tell you how many time I have heard that *it didn't do this when we tested it*, or *it worked on my machine*, when the known issues or things you needed to consider were skipped.

Adding Intelligence to your solutions

You can easily extend your application with Intelligence by using one of the Cognitive Services like:

- Search – web, visual, entity, news, custom, image, autosuggest
- Speech, speech to text, text to speech, translation, recognition

- Vision, face, content moderator, and custom vision
- Language, text analytics, translator, spell check, understanding
- Knowledge, QnA, custom decision

Had here for getting started with Cognitive Services: `https://docs.microsoft.com/en-us/azure/cognitive-services/`.

Where I have used them:

- Added speech to text for dictation in medical application
- Added search to pharmaceutical application for looking up medications

Cognitive Services SDKs packages:

- Vision: `Microsoft.Azure.CognitiveServices.Vision.ComputerVision`
- Speech: `Microsoft.CognitiveServices.Speech`
- Text: `Microsoft.Azure.CognitiveServices.Language.TextAnalytics`

As you can see they help you add learning algorithms to your applications with minimal effort.

Using Application Insights

To me, it is critical to monitor applications and detect failures before receiving a phone call from my clients. With Azure being a closed ecosystem, you will struggle to support your applications without logging in your application that can tell you what is going on. I like to leverage **Azure Application Insights** and **NLog** to help with logging in my applications; then, I can build my monitoring from there. Application Insights can be installed with most resources and gives you some insights for free, almost like the event log on a traditional server.

Application Insights provides telemetry about your app, and when things don't get right, it is good to understand that there are two main types of telemetry—raw and aggregated instances. Aggregated data includes the counts of events per unit of time or averages. Now, it is good to understand the following categories of collected data:

- Dependencies
- App Requests
- Exceptions
- Page Views

- Performance counters
- Log Traces
- Custom Events

Application Insights also has the ability for smart detection and raises issues automatically. It also can provide a Live Metric stream for up-to-date metrics on your app and application maps that show all the connection points. But the biggest piece, at least for me, is the analytics you can gain from SQL-like queries of the data it has collected. You can view the raw data or you can visualize it in charts and graphs. The telemetry data is also available in Visual Studio for debugging and such. Take some time to learn more about Application Insights, as it will most likely pay for itself on first use. For more information, go to `https:/ /docs.microsoft.com/en-us/azure/application-insights/`.

Leveraging on-premises resources

Now, in some application development scenarios, there may be a need to reach back into an organizations network to get data. There are many ways to accomplish this, and each has its merits, such as exposing services, writing to queues (relaying), VPNs, or Azure Express Route. Each choice has it pros and cons, but I recommend using a secure VPN/Express Route. This, however, has one BIG stipulation: you need to use dynamic routing. If you use static routing, this is not supported. VPN solutions come with a premium cost but are worth it in my eyes, as they allow Azure resources to interact with on-premise resources, like the data on the internal network. But, you should really understand your needs before venturing down this trail.

Most developers make the mistake that they need to move everything to Azure when hybrid solutions may be more in line. This becomes apparent with larger enterprise-based systems that are not in Azure or good candidates for moving to Azure. But, creating a secure way to access these resources is paramount. When considering how to build your hybrid solution, there are three security models you should consider:

1. **Synchronized**: Is the simplest and quickest method, and may require the user to maintain two passwords unless you sync the hash of the user's password with an on-premises AD.
2. **Pass-through**: Is a simple password validation against your on-premises AD, hence AAD passes the sign-in validation to an on-premises AD directly.
3. **Federated**: Is an SSO solution that allows the user to authenticate using on-premises credentials for an Azure resource using the ADFS infrastructure to achieve high availability and scale, which allows you to simplify management with the Azure portal.

Each of these options has their merits, so really consider how you want to approach this and review the pros and cons of each before choosing a path.

Summary

Development in Azure is not completely different for traditional development, with some caveats. We discussed the benefits of using Dependency Injection in your development. Hopefully, we started you on the trail to developing solid solutions in Azure, as well as stressing the importance of security and logging. We also reviewed how to leverage on-premises resources in our journey.

Now that we have some basis for development, let's look at the how DevOps fits into this process.

Questions

Let's take a look at what we have learned:

1. What is DI?
2. What is MVC?
3. What is FMA? Why is it important?
4. What is B2C?
5. What does RBAC mean?
6. Do you have to check for NULL in Setter Injection?
7. What is a mock?

Further reading

- Azure documentation: https://docs.microsoft.com/en-us/azure/

6
Deploying Solutions to Azure

Now that we have gained an understanding of developing solutions for Azure, how do we deploy these solutions? In this chapter, we will learn what you need to know about deploying solutions in Azure. We will approach this using DevOps, which can sit on top of any Agile process you wish to use for your development processes.

The following topics will be covered in this chapter the following:

- Deploying to Azure
- Testing deploys
- Using deployment slots
- Deploying infrastructure

Technical requirements

The requirements for this chapter are:

- **Azure DevOps:** `http://dev.azure.com/`
- **Package artifacts:** `https://docs.microsoft.com/en-us/azure/devops/artifacts/index?view=vsts`

Deploying solutions in Azure

As we enter this new work of compute as a utility and the only limit is our budget, organizations want better and broader collaboration between their teams. They also want quicker, faster, leaner delivery of software and infrastructure solutions, and as the environment and development changes, that we have an evolutionary process. With deployments to Azure, you will most likely need your releases to now only infrastructure and development, but testing elements to validate the deployments were successful. The main targets you want to achieve are smaller and quicker releases while automating as much as possible. You should also try to test code from unit to functional testing, while automating this as well.

We will learn about Azure DevOps in steps.

What is DevOps?

DevOps is a software development method that emphasizes communication, collaboration, integration, automation, and a measure of cooperation between solution developers and IT professionals. As you can see in the following diagram, the method introduces a good process flow between developers and operations:

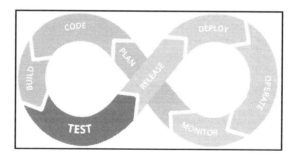

DevOps flow

So what makes DevOps different than all the other software delivery methodologies we have used. To begin with, DevOps began as a software development method meant to drive an increased velocity in the building, testing, and release of software by getting two main groups – **Developers (Dev)** and **Operations (Ops)** to work together more effectively. DevOps can be used in conjunction with your Agile or lean methodologies as it is not a replacement for these processes but an enhancement. It is meant to help guide as much automation as possible in the spirit of speed and quality, while helping to refine your operational flow for better velocity.

Above all, it's a culture thing!

What is this culture change we talk about? Let's review what DevOps is:

- It is less about what we do and more about how we do it, which means it is about how work gets done, and how people interact with each other
- It is not an off-the-shelf boxed solution that can just be implemented, there is no one-size-fits-all approach – it is implementation
- It is everyone's job, not an individual effort
- The process is more about people and less about how much "stuff" can be forced down the pipeline

Some tips for the DevOps journey:

- It's about trust – development and operations teams being segregated from one another and not being enabled to communicate, let alone collaborate, effectively
- Understand the people – try to understand ourselves first and then those around us
- Stop the blame game
- Embrace failure and learn
- Focus on bottlenecks and flow – don't be afraid to rethink your process or find a new pair of eyes to see the things you can't because you are too close
- Eliminate unplanned work – if the culture is to keep doing things that are breaking and broken, it's tough to put aside the hours outside of the firefighting to make things happen
- Be continuous
- Create cross-functional teams
- Embrace transparency
- Build mastery and purpose – a single goal everyone can focus on

The reason this is important to me is because DevOps solves some delivery issues. The development and operations of the people who deliver the software are gauged on separate results, as you can see in the following table:

Development resources are gauged on:	Operations resources are gauged on:
• Feature delivered after manual unit test on development systems	• Code delivered with little to no concern about infrastructure concern
• Rewarded mainly on timely delivery	• Reward mainly for uptime
• Development systems not the same as production	• Left with solving security issues
• Little to no concern about infrastructure/deployment impact related to code changes	• Left with solving monitoring of the application with little to no knowledge of the application
• Little to no feedback on changes until later in the software cycle	• Usually engaged at the tail end of the application development cycle

As you can see, it was almost as if we were actually pitted against each other, causing an uphill battle with each group throwing grenades in the form of tasks and each not really understanding the reason behind the urgency of the tasks. Here are some important attributes that are needed to help bridge this gap:

- Release management
    - More in-depth understanding of risks, dependencies, compliance issues

- Release/deployment coordination
    - Better tracking of discrete activities, more consistent/faster escalation of issues, a documented process control, and reporting

- Release/deployment automation
    - More consistent and repeatable processes that can be automatically invoked and executed with or without (non-production) an approval process

Why is this important regarding to solutions in Azure? With Azure being a deviation from common infrastructure practices, both from a fundamental perspective but also from a process perspective, the DevOps culture change works in tandem with the Azure culture change. This provides a new way of software delivery and the tooling help provides more consistency to the change. While DevOps isn't holistically about tooling, Azure provides a decent set of DevOps tools and processes for release management. This allows you to either fully automate the delivery of your software all the way to production, or set up semi-automated processes with approvals and on-demand deployments for any platform. Azure DevOps provides these main areas that help support these processes in one software package:

- Azure boards
- Azure repos
- Azure pipelines
- Azure artifacts
- Azure test plans

Azure Boards

To me, source control of your code not only protects your source but helps control changes to that source, but this truly fails in comparison to the business process management that helps define these changes before they happen. **Azure Boards** is the place you plan and track your project deliverables. Azure Boards provides the following:

- **Boards**: The flow of work for the team
- **Work Items**: Items to be completed by an individual
- **Backlogs**: Plan, organize, and prioritize work for the team
- **Sprints:** Time frame to complete work
- **Queries:** Filter criteria for work items or bulk updating
- **Plans:** A way to review deliverables

These are shown here in the following figure:

Azure Boards screen

All of the these are visualized within Azure Boards, which then leads us to how do we manage the code changes. Azure Repos provides code repositories to store source code and name the changes/version of that source code. These to me are the biggest features within Azure DevOps, as they are designed to protect the code and the meeting of the business process. Building a backlog and mapping out tasks helps everyone understand the deliverables and tasks being completed to meet those deliverables and then protect the code behind those deliverables. Now, this book holistically isn't about requirement gathering and project makeup. I wanted to take some time to review these events as I believe they are just as important as building the solutions. With this, let's talk about some things that will impact our development of the solution in Azure—protecting our source code. Let's look at a simplified flow the process code should take, shown here in the following diagram:

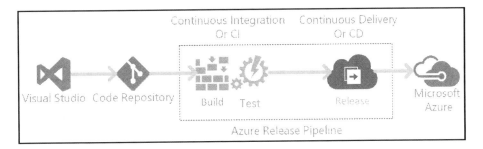

Simplified code flow with CI/CD

I prefer Git and the GitFlow process for my repository, as the pull request or PR process allows for better code review of changes being checked in the main branch. Now, branching structures can be a religious battle, but I prefer to keep it simple with the main and release strategy GitFlow offers out of the box. Even as a single developer model, I use this as it helps me keep myself honest. Let's take a quick look at how this plays out for the development process. The following diagram shows the pieces that are in play:

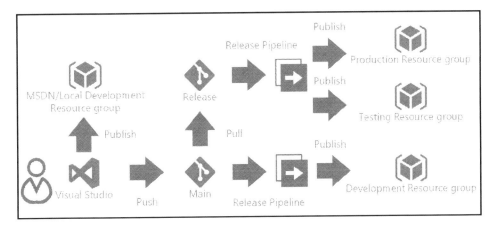

Development process flow

Learn more about Azure Boards at `https://azure.microsoft.com/en-us/services/devops/boards/`.

Azure Artifacts

Now, **Azure Artifacts** is the package you share across applications, such as npm and NuGet. I leverage them a significant amount over include 3rd party binaries directly, meaning the old `lib` folder in the source code with references to the `dlls`. When you use this process, it allows Azure Pipeline to restore/update the packages and deploy proper versions based on the `package.json` file in each project. I also recommend that if you have internal frameworks, that you package them and provide them through a feed, as you can see here in the following diagram:

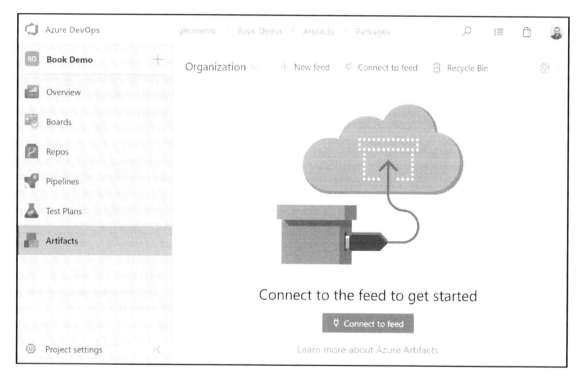

Artifact dashboard and feed

If you would like to learn more about building your own package manager, you can get more information at `https://docs.microsoft.com/en-us/azure/devops/artifacts/index?view=vsts`.

Azure Pipelines

Azure DevOps Release Pipelines should have a flow that provides feedback on the state of the code to the individual developers checking in the code. This feedback should come in as quickly as possible and code check ins should be small and iterative. You should have your teams refrain from checking in larger amounts of code covering a large number of requirements; smaller check ins are easier to handle and adjust to. This will help reduce the merging process, however, teams should always do one pull for the latest code. Let's look at the sequence diagram of this process, as shown in the following diagram:

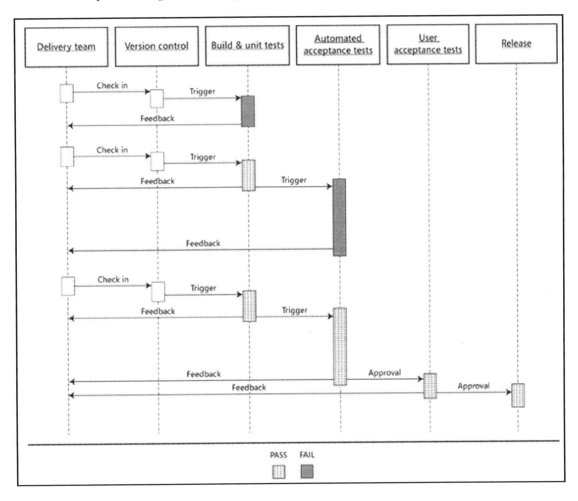

Release pipeline sequence diagram

Pipelines can not only deploy code but infrastructure as well, and are referred to as your CI/CD process. **Continuous Integration** (**CI**), is the process of developers checking in code, running tests, and receiving feedback based on the stability of the code being checked in. This process is integral as providing feedback this early in the process helps provide better overall code quality and more predictable build/test models, which means not relying on developer machines and hearing *well, it works on my machine*. **Continuous Delivery** (**CD**), is the process that ensures your code is in a shippable state and you will use it to deploy source automatically to the configured environment. So, to sum this up, CI is the process that creates the artifacts to deploy and CD is the process to deploy them.

To start using Azure Pipelines, you will need to ensure the following:

- You have an organization created in Azure DevOps
- Your source control is in a repository that Azure DevOps can access

This will be the biggest part of your interaction with Azure DevOps and to me, the most fun. There is nothing like creating a process to automatically deploy your source code, once you check it in and tests have been completed. Once this is complete, you can create tests to validate the code that was just deployed. You can create your first pipeline in Azure DevOps at `https://docs.microsoft.com/en-in/azure/devops/pipelines/get-started-yaml?view=vsts`.

Azure Test Plans

One of the biggest things I think is overlooked in most software development is testing. Testing is an art most developers don't master nor understand. What I mean by that is they will test the code in accordance with how it was written. Azure Test Plans helps with the following:

- Unit and functional testing
- Continuous testing
- Stakeholder feedback
- Exploratory and manual testing
- Performance testing

The start of this process begins with unit testing and can lead to some functional testing to gain early and quick feedback. Pushing to a test environment can also help with gaining stakeholder feedback faster and allow course corrections more quickly. So, if you want to keep your changes smaller to allow for faster delivery of code then this process will help.

Now, this isn't a book on testing so the more you automate lower in the development cycle, the more exploratory and performance testing time is available. I would like to point out that performance testing is more about code performance over the traditional *testing the infrastructure* to know when to order more *things* to help it run. Azure provides a large amount of scalability immediately over having to wait to order. So, your performance side focuses more on code than on infrastructure.

How I use Azure DevOps

I usually start by creating an organization project at `https://dev.azure.com/`, then turn over the backlog to the business side of the house with a model of **Epic – Features – Tasks**, with the tasks being entered by the developers. I work with the business team to create a good overall definition of *done* for tasks, so the developers will understand how things are considered complete. I then create a repository for code, usually in Git, as I prefer the overall process of code merging. This does come with the caveat of the team understanding the process of PRing code and how to fetch the latest code changes before checking in to help minimize the collisions in code check in. Earlier, I included how the backlog looks, but let's look at how we get to the rest of the project setup. When you log in to the DevOps portal (`https://dev.azure.com`), you will need to select your organization and the project within that organization, as you can see in the following screenshot:

Azure DevOps dashboard

Once you select the project, you will then see the Azure DevOps menu structure and we need to create a repository for the code. I usually try to keep my repositories as small and as manageable as I can, only placing code needed. I use NuGet for shared code and third party libraries to simply dependencies. As you can see here, in the following diagram, create your repository or repositories needed to support the code development:

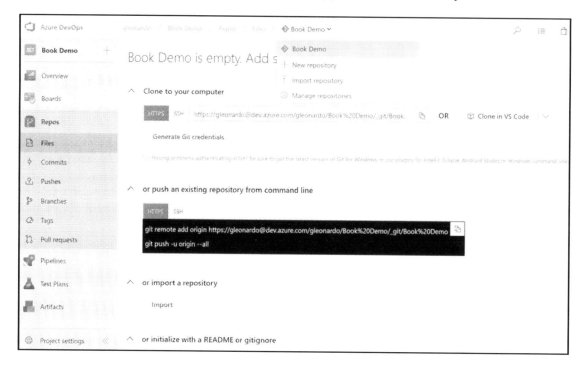

Create a repository in Azure DevOps

I generally use HTTPS for Windows-based machines and SSH for Linux-based machines for repository cloning. For those who don't know, cloning is creating a *local* copy of the only repository and branching is create a working copy of the code to work on. The code being worked on will use a pull request or PR to merge the code back into the CI main branch. This helps so that you can have an extra set of eyes to review the code by a different team member before it is checked in, formerly called a *code review*. The PR process includes a build and an automated run of unit testing, then the merge happens.

Once your code repository in main is updated with a PR, your release pipeline should take over and build, then release your code to your development integration environment. This release or future releases can be released to QA or production with the same targeted build by either a manual/automated release with approvals. Let's see how a build would look, shown here in the following diagram:

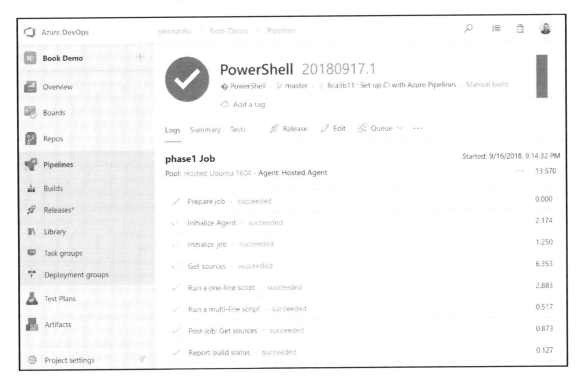

Build view

For your `azure-pipelines.yml` file, the acceptable pool values are as follows:

```
pool:
vmImage: 'Ubuntu 16.04' # other options: 'macOS 10.13',
'VS2017-Win2016'
```

Once the builds are completed, you can now build out your release, as you can see in the following diagram. Now, I would like to note that there is not a one size fits all for pipelines, as they should contain all the necessary pieces to deploy an application:

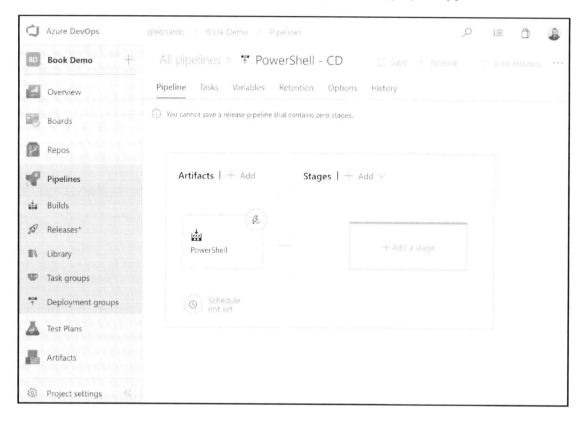

Azure Pipelines release

So at the end of the day, I like my builds and releases to be phased, meaning I run the infrastructure part, the code deploys part, then the tests. I like to ensure I build out my PR and CI build process upfront as well, as my release process to automatically deploy at least to my development integration environment.

What are deployment slots?

Deployment slots are parallel containers that exist within an Azure resource, such as App Services. These slots can be used as *environments*, such as staging, QA, or dev. I leverage slots as a staging environment that can be used to *test* code being deployed in a production environment. Once you are done with your verification testing, you can switch slots for zero downtime. Now, as I mentioned, you can use them for QA and dev environments but this can create issues with downstream resources such as databases or services. I always prefer and recommend keeping a division between environments, for data security, access, and so on, as you can see in the following daigram:

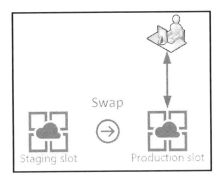

Deployment slots

Deployment slots:

- They act like an App Service instance
- The main slot is referred to as the production slot
- They can leverage the configuration of App Services
- They are scaled by App Service Plan and are not separate
- The pricing is included with the App Service Plan
- They have their own URL and site extensions

You can create a deployment slot, as you can see in the following screenshot. Remember, this is only available if they are included in your App Service plan:

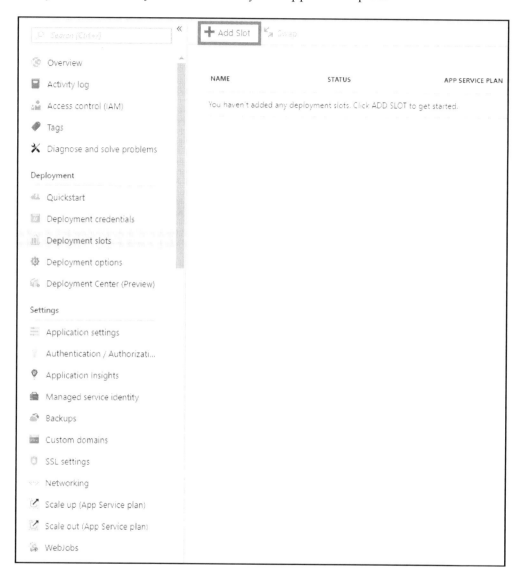

Create a deployment slot

The big benefit of using deployment slots is that you can roll back a deployment if needed, quickly and easily.

You need to remember the following when swapping. It changes the following:

- IP Address (always changes)
- Publishing endpoints
- Custom domain names
- SSL certificates and bindings
- Scale settings
- Webjob schedulers (if used)
- Site extensions

Now, I would like to point out that you can, which I do not recommend, turn on Auto Swap in your application settings in Azure. The setting to do so is shown in the following screenshot, with a note that this cannot be done with production slots:

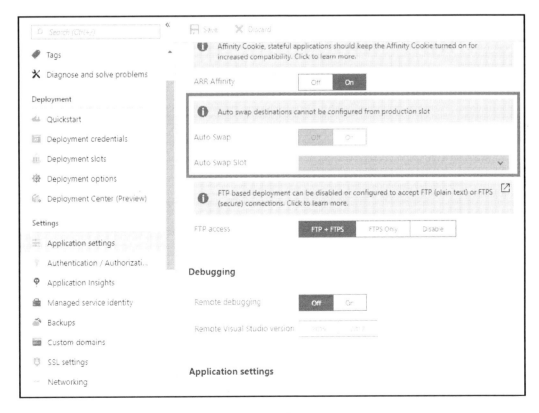

Turn on Auto Swap

One of the biggest benefits of using slots in production is that you can use the **testing in production** feature. This allows you to direct a percentage of your traffic to the slot to fully test code changes in production. This can give you an *extra* layer of testing and monitoring your application, and provide unique insight before you open the floodgates for your changes. I highly recommend using this for your overall sanity. Let's see how we configure it, as shown in the following screenshot:

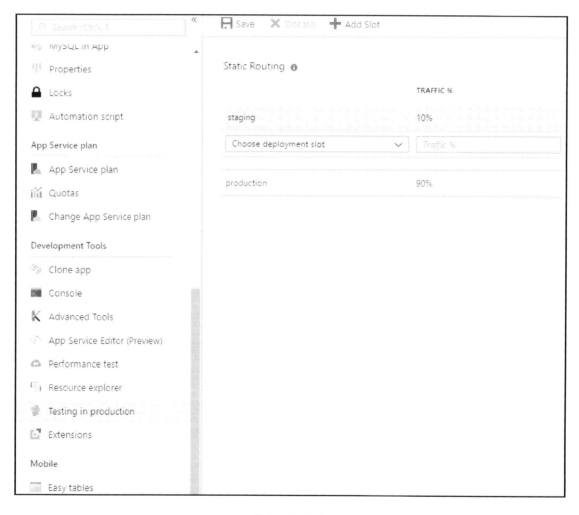

Testing in production

As you can see in the following diagram, we are directing 10% of our production users to the new slot and because it is its own App Service container, we can monitor it separately from the main production slot, which is pretty cool:

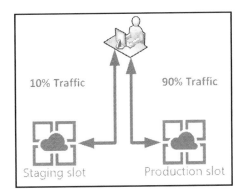

Testing in production summary

So, as you can see, deployment slots offer to allot and can be leveraged from Azure DevOps pipelines and other deployment mechanisms. But, let's review the pros and cons:

Pros:

- Zero-downtime code deploys
- Testing in production feature
- Great to verify code deploys in the exact environment

Cons:

- Are considered *new App Services*, so extensions and configurations need to redeployed
- Based on App Service Plan, need Standard or above to use
- Because they are based on the App Service Plan, they don't scale separately

How Azure helps with DevOps

Now, you can also use the Deployment Center link in the menu structure to connect to your or third party source repository to deploy, as well as from the Azure Portal. Now, I would only use this if you needed a quick POC deployment over a traditional process, but I did want to note and show the Deployment Center option, as we see in the following screenshot:

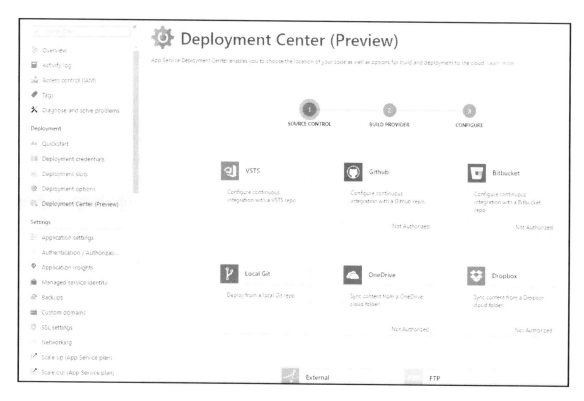

Deployment Center

This can be leveraged as a CI/CD, as things that are checked into the repository will get deployed, but as I stated, I prefer a more robust system that matches requirement to code for better overall project tracking. As you can see in the preceding figure, you can use:

- Azure DevOps (still says VSTS)
- GitHub
- Bitbucket
- Local Git
- OneDrive
- Dropbox
- External
- FTP

The Azure DevOps will create a pipeline for you in your Azure DevOps project or link to an existing one. This gives great flexibility in creating your pipeline for deployments. But again, create a process that works for you and your team that meets your goals as a group and fits within your proficiencies.

Summary

As you can see, there's a rich process and tools to help with deploying a solution in Azure. We also learned how Azure DevOps assists with bringing the two sides of the house together to help with the solution delivery. At the end of the day, there is no true silver bullet, but we can get close.

There is a key to remember on your journey to understanding:

- The journey to DevOps, above all, is a culture change
- DevOps is less about what we do and more about how we do it
- DevOps is everyone's job
- It's important to realize that more *stuff* is not the solution to a successful DevOps transition or any cultural transition for that matter

The Azure DevOps is a great tool; now let's take the opportunity to put all this together in the upcoming chapter.

Questions

Let's take a look at what we have learned:

1. What does CI stand for?
2. What makes up the word DevOps?
3. What is CD?
4. What did Azure DevOps replace?
5. What does PR mean?
6. What are the components that make up DevOps?

Further reading

- Azure documentation can be found at: https://docs.microsoft.com/en-us/azure/
- Azure DevOps can be found at: https://azure.microsoft.com/en-us/blog/introducing-azure-devops/

7
Putting It All Together

Now that my applications are in Azure, now what? How do I monitor and support them? When I have issues, how do I troubleshoot them? Let's discuss environments, Dev, QA, and Prod. How do I control the cost and estimated cost?

The following topics will be covered in this chapter:

- Monitoring and support
- Troubleshooting
- Environments and cost
- How to estimate project cost

Technical requirements

The requirements for this chapter are as follows:

- High Availability Advisor: `https://docs.microsoft.com/en-us/azure/advisor/advisor-high-availability-recommendations`
- Security Advisor: `https://docs.microsoft.com/en-us/azure/advisor/advisor-security-recommendations`
- Performance Advisor: `https://docs.microsoft.com/en-us/azure/advisor/advisor-performance-recommendations`
- Cost Advisor: `https://docs.microsoft.com/en-us/azure/advisor/advisor-cost-recommendations`
- Security Center Alerts: `https://docs.microsoft.com/en-us/azure/security-center/security-center-managing-and-responding-alerts`
- Azure Front Door: `https://docs.microsoft.com/en-us/azure/frontdoor/front-door-overview`

Our journey

As we began our journey with this book, my hopes were to keep things simple and direct while sprinkling in my experiences where needed. Being a harsh critic of myself, I feel I struggled a bit with sharing because of how fast Azure changes in reflection to the issues I had to resolve, many of which don't really exist anymore. As we journeyed, we learned about **as a Service** in reflections to resources, whether they be IaaS, PaaS, or SaaS. The first piece of this transformation is to create a cloud strategy, to cover moving your existing **resources** to the cloud, application modernization, and greenfield development. Your plan should be fluid and allow for new changes and learning. I also have learned, in addition to your cloud strategy that you should create a learning strategy to help with these new changes in Azure, as you most likely won't solve issues the same way tomorrow as you do today.

Your planning should always include a roadmap, so everyone can understand the forward movement and help with course corrections based on new findings. I try to keep three stages in mind: experimentation, transformation, and migration. Experimentation helps with the learning of how to solve a problem in Azure and I try to include all parties evolved under the DevOps structure. Transformation is about redesigning the application to better take advantage of Azure resources. An example would be using Application Insights for logging. Migration is the process of moving most resources to Azure. An example would be data repository data.

Remember some key points we have to cover:

- Fail fast, learn fast, meaning try many and then use the best
- Push the boundaries by taking advantage of cloud capabilities
- Use data-driven decisions by using telemetry to gain insight
- Simplify
- Communicate early and often as transparency is key

In previous chapters, we learned about tenants, subscriptions, and resource groups and then headed to architecture. From there, we covered some development and DevOps. At this point, we have our application in Azure and we need to look at how we can manage and support it. Azure has quite a few powerful tools that have matured over time. When I first got into Azure, one of the best-leveraged tools and one I still believe is underutilized is dashboards.

Dashboards

Azure dashboards are resources that are represented as JSON behind the scenes, which means the top level properties are ID, name, location, and tags. However, these don't really have much to do with dashboards.

> The type property for all dashboards is `Microsoft.Portal/dashboards` and the location property indicates the primary geographic location that stores the dashboard JSON because dashboards do not have a runtime component.

The `properties` object contains two elements, called `lenses` and `metadata`. Lenses contain the parts of the dashboard and metadata is for future features. Input values are also allowed for the dashboard component, such as the App Service or VM that are supplying the data. Let's take a look at a dashboard in Azure in the following screenshot:

Azure Dashboard

When I started using Azure dashboards, I had to create a new one each time I changed what I wanted to display between environments, for Dev, QA, and Prod. This was very difficult to manage and support; however, as you can see in the preceding screenshot, there is an ability to upload/download and clone. They can also be shared with groups or individuals. In the following screenshot, you will see what happens when you edit a dashboard. This is where you can add components to the dashboard from the side menu. I always include a text/HTML component to add some free text information:

Editing a dashboard

There is also the ability to add a component to dashboards as you review resources by pinning them. To pin, you will click on the thumbtack icon of the component you want to add. Make sure you have the dashboard selected that you want to pin to before pinning the component. In the following screenshot, let's see how this is done:

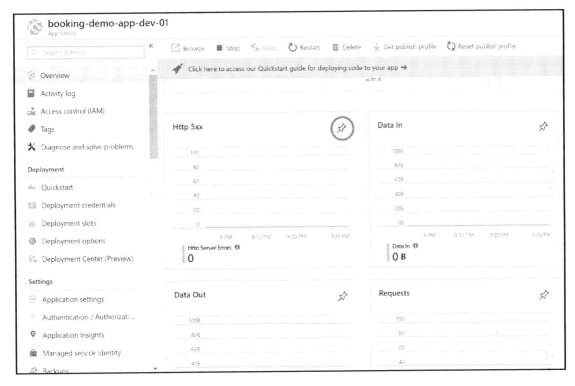

Pinning a component in Azure Portal

Once you click on it, it will add it to the active dashboard. Let's see what that looks like in the following screenshot:

Pinned component on a dashboard

As you can see, dashboards are extremely powerful visual elements in Azure that can provide quick landing pads for important application visualization elements, such as errors, data usage, and cost. Now, we can dive deeper into application support by using the Azure Advisors. Let's see how.

Azure Advisors

In Azure, there are Advisors that assist in helping you follow best practices. They are like little helpers that move through your applications in Azure and provide some great feedback on issues before they become a problem. They do this by analyzing your configurations and telemetry data and making recommendations.

Azure Advisors assist with the following errors:

- High availability
- Security
- Performance
- Cost

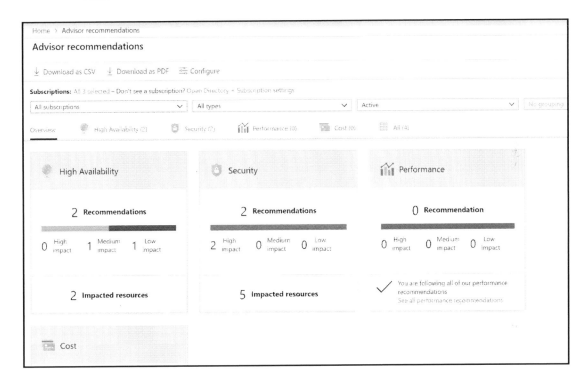

Azure Advisors

To access Azure Advisors, you need to be in the **Owner**, **Contributor**, or **Reader role** within the **Subscription**.

High Availability Advisor

This handles business-critical applications to ensure and improve continuity. It will help with recommendations, such as the following:

- Virtual Machine, Application Gateway, and availability set fault tolerance
- Virtual Machine disk performance and reliability
- Virtual Machine accidental data deletion
- Creating alerts for Azure issues that affect your resources

High Availability Advisor

As you can see, it can provide some insight into certain things that might have been missed when you configured the resources. For example, you can see in the preceding screenshot that I skipped **soft delete** for my storage. All you need to do is click on the recommendation and it will walk you to the area you need to correct; in this case, a setting.

Security Advisor/Security Center

This tab integrates with the Azure Security Center that helps detect, prevent, and respond to security threats. In the following screenshot, you can see the **Security** tab. I leverage the **Security** tab as much as I can to double-check my resources in Azure:

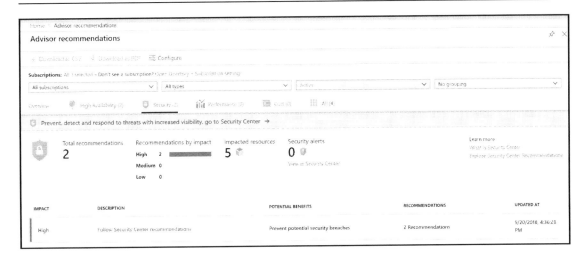

Security Advisor

In the Azure Security Center, you want to pay attention to the severity of the issue(s). You can drill into the issue by double-clicking on the issue, and, as with the other advisor, it will take you to the point where you can fix the issue:

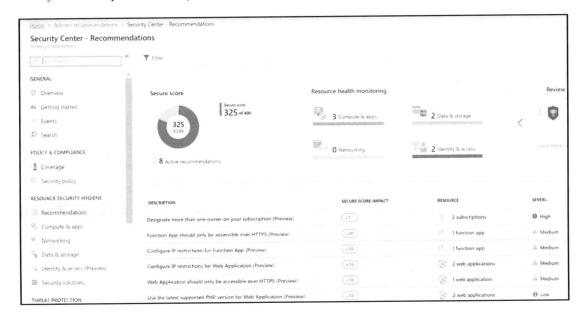

Security Center

To learn more about the Security Center, head to `https://docs.microsoft.com/en-us/azure/security-center/security-center-recommendations`. Depending on your organization needs, you will find what you need. I use the Azure Security Center for setting up policies and monitoring security, as well as to set up alerts. For more info on Security alerts go to `https://docs.microsoft.com/en-us/azure/security-center/security-center-managing-and-responding-alerts`.

You would use Azure Security Center for the following:

- Managing security policy settings with defined desired configurations of workloads and compliance.
- Monitoring security health to monitor your Azure resources
- Applying cloud defenses that provide adaptive app controls and file integrity monitors
- Managing security solutions
- Investigating threats
- Automating security workflows

I recommend leveraging as much as you need, to help secure your applications and infrastructure.

Performance Advisor

The **Performance Advisor** provides performance recommendations to help import the responsiveness of your resources. I use it mostly to review VMs and App Services performance and reliability. I usually monitor memory and CPU exhaustion and database performance. I use it to check for the following on my App Services:

1. When more memory is consumed than expected
2. When more CPU is consumed than expected
3. When a socket resource is exhausted
4. When backup fails
5. When deployment happens

The blade for this is pretty simple and follows the same drill in clicking as other Advisors. A view of the blade is shown in the following screenshot:

Performance blade

Cost Advisor

This Advisor is pretty self-explanatory and is probably the most useful one as you learn Azure. It will make recommendations based on the consumption of your resources. There is more to drill into here and you will need to set up a Cloudyn account. **Cloudyn** is Azure's Cost Management tool and it helps you to do the following:

- Monitor cloud spend
- Drive organizational accountability
- Optimize cloud efficiency

You will be directed to `https://azure.cloudyn.com/web-app2/#/azure-registration/intro` to create the connection. You will need to be an administrator and subscription owner to configure it, as you can see in the following screenshot:

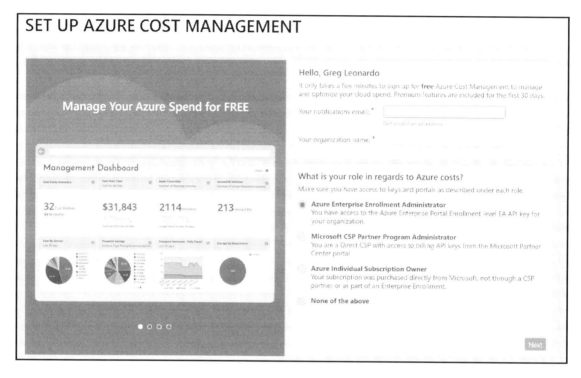

Cloudyn setup

I can't stress enough the importance of keeping an eye on your burn as you learn about Azure. So, let's look at how we monitor resources and cost in Azure.

Monitoring

An effective monitoring strategy is an essential part of the journey in Azure. **Monitoring** in Azure comprises of a group of individual services that come together to deliver comprehensive telemetry about your applications and resources in Azure. These services can also span to on-premise to provide a single source of truth for your monitoring. Monitoring fits into a few categories.

Let's take a look at them.

- Core capabilities, which include Azure Monitor, Advisor, Service Health, and Activity Log
- Shared capabilities, which include Dashboards, Alerts, and Metric Explorer
- Infrastructure capabilities, which include network monitoring, Service Map, Management Solutions, and Log Analytics.
- Application capabilities, which include Application Insights

Let take a moment to look into each of them, so we can better understand how we can use them.

Core capabilities

Core monitoring provides fundamental core telemetry monitoring across Azure resources and requires minimal configuration to use. Azure Monitor provides metrics, activity logs, and diagnostic logs for all Azure services. These are great little starting points for issues. Let's look at the **Activity Log**, shown in the following screenshot, as we have already covered the Azure Advisor:

Activity Log

The **Activity Log** is where you usually will start when things don't go 100% right. You can also find the other useful monitoring and support resources in your Azure resources at the bottom of the resource menu, as shown in the following screenshot:

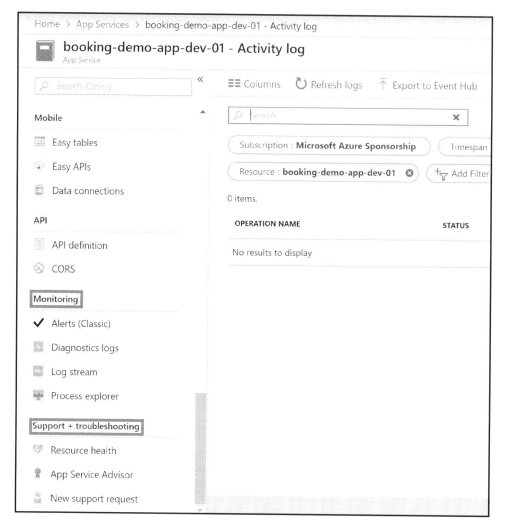

Monitoring and support in resources

There are very useful tools for supporting your Azure resources. I have leveraged Log Stream to help diagnose issues in Azure but this is a tough way to find things as it displays the active event loggings as they happen. This is why it is important to include logging in your application to make it easier to troubleshoot.

Shared capabilities

We have already discussed dashboards and how important I feel they are, but I believe another underutilized part of monitoring is alerting. I put alerts around everything I can, include third-party integration endpoints which I learn the hardware when went go sideways. Alerting is based on action groups, which contain a unique set of recipients and actions in response to an alert. Alerts can be created under various scenarios and rules. I like to find out things before my clients do. You can read more about alerting at `https:// docs.microsoft.com/en-us/azure/monitoring-and-diagnostics/monitoring-overview- unified-alerts`. Let's take a quick look at how easy it is to set up an alert.

Head to the **Alerts** blade under the **Monitor** link, and then select the **Alert** menu option, as you can see in the following screenshot:

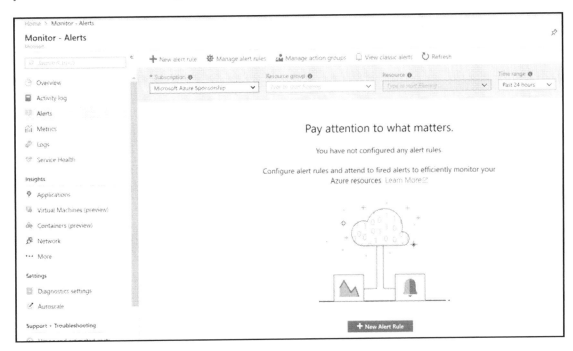

Monitoring Alert blade

You then select **+ New alert rule**, then **+ Select source**, and choose options to display the source. In this case, it is an **App Service**, as you can see in the following screenshot:

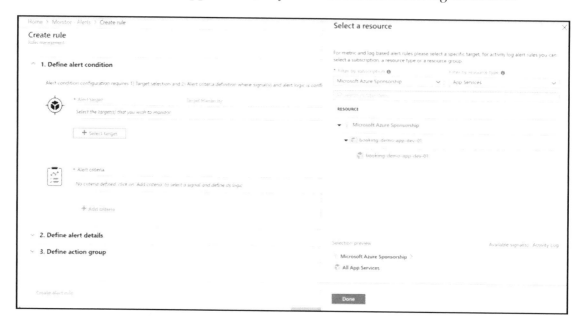

Creating an alert and selecting the source

Then select **+ Add criteria**, and then select **All Http Error**, as you can see in the following screenshot, and then click **Done**:

Adding criteria for an alert

Click on **2. Define alert details** and add your alert details, as you see in the following screenshot:

Alert details

We then click on **Define action group**, where you can select an existing one or create a new one, as you can see in the following screenshot.

You can create action types of the following:

- Email/SMS/Push/Voice
- Azure Function
- Logic App
- Webhook
- ITSM
- Automation Runbook

Defining your action group

As you can see, alerts are highly configurable and extremely useful, so I recommend using them as much as possible and even integrating them into your support system to create tickets.

Infrastructure capabilities

Log Analytics is a great tool for providing a single repository of the collected data by Azure monitoring. Even Application Insights and Security Center can store their data within Log Analytics, which can be its analytics engine on the data. Management solutions are a set of logic that are packaged to support a particular resource in Azure, such as a container or SQL monitoring. Management solutions rely on Log Analytics to store and analyze the data. There are other monitors that work with various aspects of your network resources. Let's take a quick look at them:

- Network Watcher, which is scenario-based monitoring and uses Azure metrics to store data
- Network Performance Monitor, which monitors your connectivity to other environments
- Express Route Monitor, which is used to monitor you Express Route circuits.
- DNS Analytics, used for stats on your Azure DNS traffic.
- Service Endpoint Monitor, which tests the endpoints and detects service issues
- Service Map is a pretty cool, as it visualizes your resources and their dependencies.

Application capabilities

Application Insights is the main tool for applications. It can also be configured to trap telemetry by default. As I explained before, leveraging this with NLog provides great logging support with minimal effort. You can also leverage it in your alerting strategy and you can use the Analytic tools to visualize the queries in graphs. The default blade is shown in the following screenshot:

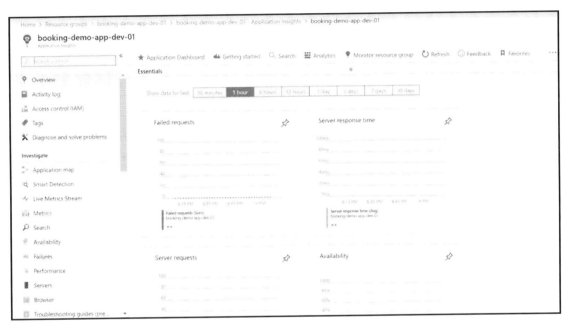

App Insights blade

I generally use the Analytics portion to run queries against my data store for both informational and support purposes. You can also look at overall application performance and alert on performance issues as well. Let's look at the Analytics dashboard, as shown in the following screenshot:

Analytics dashboard

Ask you can see, there are quite a few Insights available. I general mostly use exceptions, traces, **customEvents**, **performanceCounters**, and **customMetrics**. One of the coolest features is the integration with Visual Studio, but I could spend an entire book on Application Insight and its uses. For further reading on this, head to `https://docs.microsoft.com/en-us/azure/application-insights/`.

Advanced topics

I would like to reiterate a few things. You use App Service Environments or ASE/Isolated App Services if you have GDFR or PII data requirements. Also, ensure you use TDE in your data stores out the gate to help protect your data. If you are developing mobile applications, I would use Xarmarin, as writing in C# and deploying to all platforms is pretty sweet.

At the time of writing this book, some new features in Azure became available that I would like to discuss. The first one is **Azure Front Door** and the second one is **Azure confidential computing**. Let's take a look at what these have to offer.

What is Azure Front Door?

Azure Front Door is a layer 7 or HTTP/HTTPS layer anycast protocol. It was designed to define, manage, and monitor global traffic routing in high availability global (multi-regional) scenarios. It helps accelerate your application performance by using a TCP-based `anycast` protocol that connects a site user to the nearest **Point of Presence** (**POP**), in order to improve application performance. It assists with smart health probes to monitor backend latency and availability, providing automatic failover if the backend goes down. This can also be used in maintenance scenarios. It also assists with URL routing and multi-site hosting, as well as SSL off-loading. This is key for me as it solved the App Service Cert issues with the subscription boundaries. Azure Front Door is a premium service and comes at a price. I have not had a chance at the time writing of writing this book to use it in a production environment but thought I would share what I have learned so far, but you can learn more at `https://docs.microsoft.com/en-us/azure/frontdoor/front-door-overview`. This, like all other services, I would use when needed, especially if you need global distribution.

What is Azure confidential computing?

I wanted to take some time to mention a cloud-first data initiative that I have not had the pleasure of working with yet. The Azure confidential computing efforts have led to the creation of **Trusted Execution Environments** (**TEEs**). These are containers that protect the data from being accessible from an outside source. Microsoft worked at following these principles:

- Migration of top data breach threats
- The customer is in full control of data, rest, transit, or use
- The code runs in a verified/protected environment

This also allows customers to share and use AI against data to reach better conclusions.

The biggest point to the Advanced section is building solutions in Azure, which requires constant learning as part of your strategy. Things around computing are going to change fast; so make sure you have walked a mile in those shoes before using the new changes.

Quick tips on Azure estimating and cost control

As you begin your journey with Azure, you should work at estimating the resources you intend to use in Azure. This will help keep you on the right track and also help with budgeting for your services. I try to approach this in the following way:

- Put together the expectations you plan to achieve. This will help keep you on the right path.
- You need to know the apps you are moving and creating. Understand the dependencies, creating sequence diagrams, and flow between resources. This helps with using the Azure pricing calculator.
- I like to prototype, which allows me to test and assess my resources.
- I keep an eye on cost and create alerts when the cost gets close to budgets. You can also put spending limits on subscriptions, but I wouldn't suggest that as once it is hit, your resources will stop working.
- I recommend using tags on your resources to group and monitor data., which can also be alerted on. I leverage this more when I want to track billing by the department so I can charge to their budget.
- Use the Azure Cost Advisor to help review burn and adjust costs.
- Use development and code to help estimate; for example, CosmosDB code snippets to get the cost of a query for estimating.
- You can use pre-paid for your subscription to get a discount in 6-12 month increments.
- Set up an EA or CSP with Microsoft to get discounts on resources.
- Use programs, such as Partners or Bizspark, to receive free allocations by the month.
- Use free resources in non-production environments.
- If you use VMs, size them correctly for expected users. You can start low and then scale up and out.
- Instead of VMs, use PaaS resources.
- Leverage elastic pools in SQL.

Summary

We have taken some time to see how to leverage Advisors and monitors in Azure. The Advisor offers recommendations on availability, security, cost, and performance. We also looked at how monitoring and alerting can assist in supporting your resources in Azure. There were also some great tips on estimating and cost control.

Now that we have put it all together, let's review some best practices when developing solutions in Azure.

Questions

Let's take a look at what we have learned:

1. Can Azure dashboards be cloned?
2. Can Azure dashboard be uploaded or downloaded?
3. Can you pre-pay for Azure?
4. What can you use instead of VMs for services?
5. What type of Advisors are there?

Further reading

Azure documentation can be found here: `https://docs.microsoft.com/en-us/azure/`

8
Best Practices to Make Your Life Easier in Azure

Now that we have put everything together, let's look at some best practices and tips to make your life easier in Azure. In this chapter, we will cover development practices for dashboards and monitoring.

I am going to cover as many best practices as I have learned, with my focus on the most commonly used resources in Azure. I am not going to cover everything, but provide some insight into what I have learned. As we plan for Azure, we need to keep in mind the three basic stages of experimentation, migration, and transformation. To review what these are, let's look at them individually:

- **Experimentation** is what we build, how we develop it, how we test it, how we deploy it, and how we monitor and maintain it. Experimentation is constrained by the boundaries of your operations and development personnel. The main goals are to go fast, push boundaries, make data-driven decisions, simplify, and communicate.
- **Migration** is the process of moving on-premises resources to Azure workloads.
- **Transformation** is the process of maximizing applications for Azure.

There are, of course, some general things you should and shouldn't do in Azure, so let's start there first:

- First and foremost, create a cloud strategy or plan around your vision.
- Always keep it simple; complexity creates issues that can be difficult to manage in Azure.
- The more infrastructure you delegate, the better, so choose IaaS, SaaS, PaaS, or a combination.

- Have some best practices and/or architectural guidelines on hang to assist you in your journey.
- Do not try to apply on-premises architectural behaviors to cloud solutions as do not apply.

Tenant and subscriptions

The following are best practices for both tenants and subscriptions:

- Keep subscriptions to a minimum to reduce complexity
- Segment bills by leveraging tagging, instead of creating more subscriptions
- Use resource groups as application lifecycle container boundaries
- Use RBAC to grant access and to delegate administration

However, you should avoid these practices:

- Do not create a subscription for each of the development, testing, and production environments to protect quota and enforce security. Instead, leverage the features of Azure DevTest labs (an IaaS solution), App Service Slots, or opt for Azure DevTest access using an MSDN subscription (as this creates an issue with cross-subscription sharing, like wildcard App Service Certificates which are stored in Azure KeyVaults and other subscriptions can't share them).
- Do not consider enforcing quota is necessary—use **Azure Resource Manager** (**ARM**) policies to help manage quotas.
- Do not create multiple subscriptions just because you need to have separate bills for each department—tagging can be used to separate out the costs instead. Separate subscriptions introduce the need for a second layer of networking infrastructure, or for cross-subscription virtual networks through site-to-site VPNs. While it is possible to do, it does increase complexity.
- Do not use a subscription as the primary method of delegating administration. Subscriptions should be a very high-level administrative container, but that's it. However, it might make sense, for example, to have one subscription per IT department in a company with multiple IT departments.
- Avoid spanning applications across multiple subscriptions, even with multiple environments, because it reduces your ability to view and manage all the related items from one place and on one bill.

- If you have multiple subscriptions (for example, Azure DevTest access on an MSDN subscription), don't split these subscriptions by development, testing, and production; instead, split by groups of apps, with each entire app and its related apps contained within a single subscription.
- Do not proactively split subscriptions based on the fact that, eventually, you will need more resources. Resource limits are always increasing, so by the time you may get close to a present-day limit, it will likely have been increased.

Virtual machines (VMs)

Here are some things you should be following with respect to VMs:

- Protect VMs with secure authentication and access control
- Use the ARM Template for consistency in deployment
- Use multiple VMs for better availability, and consider putting them into availability sets
- Integrate VMs into Azure Security Center and use anti-malware
- Leverage Azure Monitor to help with visibility into resource issues
- Encrypt your disks

For more details, refer the MSDN documentation, available at `https://blogs.msdn.microsoft.com/plankytronixx/2015/05/01/azure-exam-prep-fault-domains-and-update-domains/`

The following practices should be avoided:

- Do not give everyone admin control, useless you use Azure Privileged Identity Management
- Do not allow VMs to get behind our their patches and updates
- Do not forget to use a key encryption key (KEK) as an extra layer of encryption.

Keep VMs with the same life cycle in the same resource groups, and use tagging to roll up billing cost to departments, if necessary.

Virtual networks

Here are some practices that should be followed in Azure, with regard to virtual networks:

- Use subnets for large IP address spaces
- Use **Network Security Groups** (**NSG**) to provide allow/deny rules for network traffic

However, it's best to avoid the following:

- Don't use split tunneling; instead, enable forced tunneling. An example of a split tunnel is like when you VPN to your corporate network from Starbucks, which you will then have access to all your corporate resources, but when you go to the internet it does not go through the VPN. When connected to a corporate network you want all your traffic to go through the VPN for security reason and to reduce risk, which is what happens when you enable forced tunneling.

 Virtual networks are the core component for making your resources secure, so plan them wisely. Implement Azure DMZ if required. While making gateway subnets, keep their scope as small as possible, to avoid IP wastage.

 The default system routes are usually all that you need, but you can create user-defined routes. The default system routes let Azure resources initiate communication between themselves, which is usually only what you need, but if you need more you can define your own user-defined routes.

Azure App Services

Generally, unless there is a true business reason, you should keep your App Services and supporting resources, such as a database, in the same region. This helps reduce latency and outbound data-transfer charges for cross-region usage.

The following are the best practices for App Services:

- Use App Services' Auto-Healing feature, like recycling when request response is slow.
- Scale up to control the number of users per instance, and scale out to control the load over the user. Scaling out can be controlled through autoscaling; however, autoscale is dependent on the pricing tier.

- Try to create your apps to be stateless to help with scaling.
- If you have GDFR or PII requirements, use App Service Environments and isolate App Services.
- Use Azure Active Directory or Azure B2C to secure your apps.
- Restrict access to need-to-know and least privileges, for both application permissions and resource permissions.

> If large media files are present, consider implementing CDN.

The following practices should be avoided:

- Do not turn on autoscaling without understanding the consequences.
- To not leverage logging your application, it is highly important you build logging into your application.
- Do not put keys or secrets in configuration files—protect your keys by using Azure Key Vault instead.

> To help control cost, pay attention to the tier options, because although they may appear to cost more per month, you may be able to run fewer instances, as you won't need to scale out as much. For instance, the PremiumV2 tier gives you a faster CPU, SSD storage, and double memory-to-core ratio, which means that you can run your apps on fewer instances.

Data stores

The following best practices should be employed for SQL databases:

- Ensure **Transparent Data Encryption (TDE)** is enabled
- Use a centralized identity management system for authentication and authorization
- Restrict access by IP, and only give access to those that need it

However, you should avoid the following:

- Don't open all IPs through your firewall

Using Azure AD gives you access to the following features:

- Single source for password rotation
- Manage permissions with groups
- **Multi-factor Authentication (MFA)**

Azure Key Store

Here are some best practices for Key Store:

- Remember to grant access at a specified scope; this can be users, groups, or applications.
- Control which users have access.
- Store your certificates in your key vault.
- Ensure you enable soft deletes to recover keys deleted in inadvertent or malicious ways.

However, the following practices should be avoided:

- Make sure that you do not leave orphaned key/secrets in your vault.

 Azure Key Vaults have a subscription boundary, meaning you can access them across subscriptions.

Azure Mobile

The following are some best practices for Mobile:

- Use MVVM pattern
- Use portal libraries
- Use three-tiered architecture
- Use constructor injection whenever possible, but when not, use static initialization

However, you should avoid doing the following:

- Do not believe performance data

Summary

There is no magic bullet for deploying solutions in Azure. Throughout this chapter, we have looked at some dos and don'ts for a few of the resources in Azure. I hope my experiences have been helpful. Remember, your journey with Azure is a marathon, not a sprint—fail fast and learn faster. Work at using a DevOps approach to Azure, and ensure you put yourself in a good position to support your resources.

Innovation hinges on the backs of the courageous, those that challenge the every day, and feel they can do it better. So, don't fear the new—get to know it.

Well, enjoy your journey to the cloud.

Questions

Let's take a look at what we have learned:

1. Can resource tagging help with assigning costs to departments?
2. What is TDE?
3. Where should you store certificates in Azure?
4. What is NSG?

Further reading

- The Azure documentation can be found at `https://docs.microsoft.com/en-us/azure/`.
- Azure Security Best Practices, available at `https://docs.microsoft.com/en-us/azure/security/security-best-practices-and-patterns`.
- Azure Network Best Practices, available at `https://docs.microsoft.com/en-us/azure/security/azure-security-network-security-best-practices`.
- Azure Identity and Access Security Best Practices, available at `https://docs.microsoft.com/en-us/azure/security/azure-security-identity-management-best-practices`.

Assessments

Chapter 1 – Getting Started with Azure

1. `https://portal.azure.com/`
2. A virtual representation of an organization and is directory-backed.
3. The first level container that contains resource groups and resources has shared boundaries
4. To contain your resources, an application life cycle container
5. Azure Resource Manager, and contains all the resources in JSON format and infrastructure-as-code
6. Desired state configuration
7. Azure Active Directory, and Azure Security Resource

Chapter 2 – Moving Existing Apps to Azure

1. Move VMs/physical servers directly to the cloud with no code change
2. Used to sync your on-premise AD
3. Azure Resource Manager
4. Yes
5. VM-backed
6. Data Transfer Unit, SQL server resource cost
7. Infrastructure-as-a-Service
8. Platform-as-a-Service

Chapter 3 – Building Solutions in Azure

1. Cheaper resources
2. SaaS AI solutions
3. 5

4. Key Vault, Express Route, App Service Certificate
5. Microservices, messaging, tiered
6. App Service Environment
7. Internet of Things

Chapter 4 – Understanding the Infrastructure behind Solutions Built in Azure

1. SDK or tool to support development
2. Azure Resource Management
3. dependsOn
4. Yes
5. Code helpers
6. Yes
7. Yes
8. Yes

Chapter 5 – Developing Solutions the Right Way in Azure

1. Dependency injection
2. Model View Controller
3. Failure mode analysis identifies errors and types
4. Business to customer
5. Role-Based access control
6. Yes
7. Helps with unit testing by injecting data in an object

Chapter 6 – Deploying Solutions to Azure

1. Continuous integration
2. Development and operations
3. Continuous delivery
4. VSTS
5. Pull request
6. Azure boards, Azure pipeline, Azure Repos, Azure Test plans, and Azure Artifacts

Chapter 7 – Putting It All Together

1. Yes
2. Yes
3. Yes
4. PaaS, or containers
5. High availability, cost, security, and performance

Chapter 8 – Best Practices to Make Your Life Easier in Azure

1. Yes
2. Transparent data encryption
3. Key vault
4. Network security group

Other Books You May Enjoy

If you enjoyed this book, you may be interested in these other books by Packt:

Hands-On Cloud Administration in Azure
Mustafa Toroman

ISBN: 978-1-78913-496-4

- Understand the concepts of IaaS and PaaS
- Learn design patterns for Azure solutions
- Design data solutions in Azure
- Explore concepts of hybrid clouds with Azure
- Implement Azure Security in cloud
- Create and manage Azure resources with script-based tools

Architecting Microsoft Azure Solutions - Exam Guide 70-535
Sjoukje Zaal

ISBN: 978-1-78899-173-5

- Use Azure Virtual Machines to design effective VM deployments
- Implement architecture styles, like serverless computing and microservices
- Secure your data using different security features and design effective security strategies
- Design Azure storage solutions using various storage features
- Create identity management solutions for your applications and resources
- Architect state-of-the-art solutions using Artificial Intelligence, IoT, and Azure Media Services
- Use different automation solutions that are incorporated in the Azure platform

Leave a review - let other readers know what you think

Please share your thoughts on this book with others by leaving a review on the site that you bought it from. If you purchased the book from Amazon, please leave us an honest review on this book's Amazon page. This is vital so that other potential readers can see and use your unbiased opinion to make purchasing decisions, we can understand what our customers think about our products, and our authors can see your feedback on the title that they have worked with Packt to create. It will only take a few minutes of your time, but is valuable to other potential customers, our authors, and Packt. Thank you!

Index

P

Performance Advisor 176
performanceCounters 188
Personally Identifiable Information (PII) 83
Platform as a Service (PaaS)
  about 9, 48, 75
  cons 75
  pros 75
PowerShell 40

R

re-architecting 33, 34
refactor 32
rehost 30
release pipeline 113
Request Units (RU/s) 93
Resource Groups (RG) 13
resources
  about 168
  creating, in Azure Portal 35
rewriting 34

S

SaaS migrations 37
Scaffolding 77
Secure Sockets Layer/Transport Layer Security
  (SSL/TLS) 65
security 122
Security Center 123, 124
security models
  federated 142
  pass-through 142
  synchronized 142
Security tab 174
Service Fabric 7, 94

service lifetimes 139
Software as a Service (SaaS)
  about 9, 75
  cons 75
  pros 75
storage accounts
  about 92
  premium 92
  standard 92
Storage Service Encryption (SSE) 92
Subscription (Sub) 13
subscriptions
  best practices 194

T

tenant
  about 5
  best practices 194
Tenant
  setting up 14
Transparent Data Encryption (TDE) 90, 121, 197
Trusted Execution Environments (TEEs) 189

V

virtual machines (VMs) 195
virtual networks 196
Virtual Private Network (VPN) 38
Visual Studio
  developing 109, 110
VNet 66

W

WordPress site
  setting up, on Marketplace 16, 21
  setting up, on Portal 16, 21

21064826R00126

Made in the USA
San Bernardino, CA
31 December 2018